HOW TO LISTEN ASSERTIVELY

BAXTER AND CORINNE GEETING

MONARCH

Originally published as
   Huh! How to Win Through Assertive Listening

Manufactured in the United States of America

10 9 8 7 6 5 4 3 2 1

ISBN 0-671-18336-2

Contents

Having dedicated a large share of my professional life to the study of dynamic listening as a vital part of management, industry, education, the professions, and all areas of human relations, I am quite naturally excited to discover a book which not only continues, but brings added dimensions to, the science of listening.

How to Listen Assertively is challenging, fresh, and very much in the modern spirit. It presents an absorbing step-by-step approach to the process of dynamic listening; goes on to take a new look at some vital skills involved in various types of listening; and concludes with a lively series of practical applications to a wide variety of life situations.

It is my hope this book will launch a much needed renaissance of interest in listening — ASSERTIVE LISTENING — as a fundamental part of all communication, capable of changing group life for the better and of contributing to the self-actualization of every human being, no matter how young, no matter how old!

Ralph G. Nichols, Ph.D.

Some Words About Words

Authors' notes on the meanings of words used in this book:

Assertive, as we use it, means:

Positive .... not Negative
Multi-Purposeful .... not Insular
Confident .... not Timid
Helpful .... not Hostile
Courageous .... not Fearful
Analytical .... not Skeptical
Friendly .... not Intimidating
Concerned .... not Indifferent
Thoughtful .... not Dogmatic
Active .... not Passive
Cooperative .... not Aggressive
Creative .... not Resigned *Etc. Etc. Etc.*

As an Assertive Person, we believe you can be self-actualizing without riding over the rights of others. You can be aware of your rights, as a listener, to full participation in communication, and by mastering techniques of assertive listening you can maintain your rights in any given situation. The Assertive Person respects others and has great self-respect as well.

Win, as we use it, means:

Advance . . . . not Prevail against
Aid . . . . not Defeat
Improve . . . . not Undermine
Direct . . . . not Follow
Assist . . . . not Subdue
Elevate . . . . not Deflate
Strengthen . . . . not Devitalize *Etc. Etc. Etc.*

To win as an Assertive Listener means to bring about changes in communication which will improve and strengthen human understanding between individuals, and individuals and groups. Winning means performing successfully as a change agent.

Part I

**Listening in
Full Color**

The Process

**Tuning In —
The Initial Impact**

One listener — ONE ASSERTIVE LISTENER — can wield the power of a monarch. Here's proof:

A major car manufacturer had just come out with a $75,000 TV commercial in which the commentator called attention to the car's remarkable acceleration speed, while viewers saw it zoom out of a driveway and vanish down the road.

One listener, a grandmother in Independence, Missouri, didn't like the message. To her way of thinking the commercial glamorized speeding.

So she sat right down and wrote a letter to the manufacturer.

"I've just listened to your new commercial," she began, "and I don't like what I hear or what I see.

"Are you trying to make us a nation of reckless speeders when our country already sacrifices thousands of lives each year in car wrecks?

"Are you trying to get us to use more gas just when we are supposed to be using less?

"Maybe just one person isn't important to you. But I'm not the only one who feels this way, I'll bet. I object to what I hear in your latest TV commercial! Faithfully, Molly T."

When the letter arrived in Detroit next day, it was scanned and went to top executives. A meeting was called within the hour. The message was read. And the commercial was ordered off the air at once.

The Process

While Molly T., in this case, decided immediately what she heard in the TV commercial was bad, and it was, most listening fails for the very same reason her listening succeeded.

The Listener Monitors The Message

Making snap judgments about what you hear is seldom the best way to react to a message.

Of course, in this case, the whole message was half a minute long. Molly T. had a perfect right to do what she did, and taking immediate action as she did may have saved lives and gas. As a result of her letter, too, this company now carefully tests and screens every commercial it has made before giving it clearance for airing. Any hidden messages are discovered before they go on the air. Even so, alert listeners often hear something that would be objectionable to hundreds of persons, and their response is carefully considered before commercials they object to are allowed to continue. One letter or phone call is considered representative of the reaction of at least 7,000 other persons!

Still, as we said, Molly T. was not the kind of listener who tunes into messages to listen in full color. She was a Black and White listener.

Polar Listening in Black and White

Assertive, skilled listeners know that in handling an incoming message they don't usually have to "take it or leave it."

Of course, if someone is talking interminably, or talking nonsense, or being boring, or being abusive, the listener may do well to stop listening. And walk away. Or talk back.

But this is seldom a good way to handle the monitoring of messages.

Most of the time, listeners simply can't judge a message when they first tune in with a For or Against reception. Messages (or programs) are seldom Good or Bad, Dull or Interesting, Right or Wrong, Black or White, True or False. If they were, listening would be a snap.

People who make sudden judgments about what they hear are usually a product of the school we call "Polar, Contrary Thinkers." They know only two ways to go. They judge incoming ideas, and almost everything else, in Black or White terms.

This approach has been trained into many of us. We expect those who like us to like everything about us, and if we register anything less than complete and unqualified agreement with a friend, he or she is apt to take our reaction personally.

Same goes for an enemy. If we react somewhat favorably to his or her message, we are considered (by friends) to be irresponsible or weak.

Polar listening, therefore, is safer.

Waiting to hear a complete thought — receiving it in full color, as we say — has risks. You risk having your own thinking changed, risk appearing indecisive, risk misunderstanding by friends and enemies. But assertive listening is not for the weak or meek. It takes strong, intelligent, stable people to handle its obvious risks.

Listening calls for spoken reactions, of course. And much about the quality of listening that has gone on is immediately evident in what the listener says.

What Polar Listeners Say

The Black and White (Polar) listener usually says things like:

"I don't agree with you at all!"

"That's not the way I see it!"

"I agree with you entirely!"

"You're absolutely wrong" or "You're absolutely right!"

The Process

Listening in Full Color

Polar listeners are trained like debaters — trained to take sides for or against.

But positive, assertive listeners listen in full color. They know the value of getting the complete message without taking sides, withholding judgment, tuning in without prejudice, before making decisions about what they have heard.

Assertive listeners are much better at communication and problem solving. They are much more creative in groups. When they speak up, others listen, because they know by experience that assertive listeners have thought through their messages before delivering them.

Most messages we receive come in a wide range of color. Part of a message, if we listen in color, will be pleasing, acceptable; part of it may be objectionable; the rest will lie somewhere between these opposites.

What Full-Color Listeners Say

Assertive, full-color listeners are experienced in their oral responses and messages. They have learned to be clear and articulate when speaking, so as to be able to take issue and disagree, or agree and commend, without having another person misunderstand. They know how to say what they really want to say without risking the loss of a friend. Assertive listeners, when the time comes for speaking, are also forceful orally. They know how and when to speak and are attentive to reactions on the part of their listeners!

Full-color listeners are the ones who say things like:

"Part of what you are saying is very acceptable to me, but I have some reservations about your ideas on . . . We need to clarify these further . . ."

"Could you review the first three points you made? I'm not sure I understand."

"I'd like to ask some questions, if I may, before I make up my mind about what you are saying."

"It's because we are such good friends, I want to fully understand your point of view. . . ."

Positive, assertive, full-color listeners are trained like discussion participants should be — to give and take, to question and to ponder, to consider, review, and adjust ideas. They generally rule out the polar view unless, as in the case of Molly T., it is a very short message which calls for immediate For or Against response.

The Process

Communication Depends on the Listener

Good messages, great ideas, can be lost to the world without assertive, full-color listeners. Often, a person with sound opinions and creative solutions is overruled in a group because of a fumbling approach, an off-key look, a poorly conceived statement. The assertive listener in the group will rescue this person's contribution and see that it has an airing.

Good listeners not only have their rights in the communication process, they have a responsibility to see that maximum communication has taken place. They can often correct or control a deteriorating meeting atmosphere, so good messages can get through. Sometimes it means they are the only ones able to see through the smog of bad human behavior. At times, they are the only ones able to overlook hair that's too long, hair that's too short, to hear the message as it is intended.

Instead of just saying No or Yes, the full-color listener keeps communication lines open, after tuning in, until the message goes through.

Summary

The first step in the process of Assertive Listening is *waiting* after tuning in to what someone has said — waiting to pass judgment until you have heard the message in full color as opposed to Black and White.

The Assertive Listener's response in the communication situation is carefully adjusted to keep emotions under control and communication lines open. (Experienced TV viewers don't "talk back to their sets" before waiting to see what is programmed, after tuning in. Sometimes, the patient viewers are agreeably surprised.)

Assertive Listeners know, however, they have the power to influence communication. They feel a responsibility to do so. They listen, act, and react with full knowledge of the way the other fellow is listening and reacting. They clear away confusion and situation smog before making decisions (tuning out) about what to receive for further consideration.

Assertive listeners feel OK about:
Waiting for the complete message in full color
Insisting on correcting faulty situations to receive it
Clarifying misunderstandings before judging messages
Avoiding almost always Black and White decisions
Assuming major responsibility for success in any communication

**Adjusting the
Sound —
Words and
Meanings**

What joy, power, and tragedy can rest on the understanding of a single word!

It was July, 1945.

The Emperor of Japan was ready, and his cabinet almost prepared, to accept the ultimatum of the Allies agreed on at Potsdam — give up or be crushed — but a little more time was needed to discuss terms.

A message was sent over foreign wires by the Japanese in which they announced they were following a policy of "mokumatsu." They meant a policy of "no comment."

But, in translation, the message read, "THE CABINET IGNORES THE DEMAND TO SURRENDER." "Ignores" was a second meaning of the word "mokumatsu."

The Japanese felt to recall the message would be a loss of face. So it went uncorrected.

Bombs on Hiroshima and Nagasaki, with the loss of thousands of civilian lives, and a devastating Korean war that cost the lives of thousands of American and Japanese sons, resulted. A haunting uneasiness between our two countries persisted for years afterward. All because of *one* misinterpreted word.

Words mean different things to different people. Usually, the speaker knows what he or she means by a word. Seldom can the listener know for sure what the speaker intended, even when they are communicating in the same language.

The Listener's Meaning is What Counts

It is the listener's meaning that counts, and it is up to the assertive listener to clarify meanings by asking good questions, by repeating ideas to make sure they have been received as intended, and by making certain of words when pronunciations may differ.

Strange things have happened as a result of misunderstood pronunciations. Many years ago Grandfather Fessenden, from Glasgow, Scotland, came to this country as a watchmaker. Hearing of an opening in his profession in Ottumwa, Iowa, he purchased a railroad ticket. Unfortunately, the train agent misunderstood him and sold him a ticket to Onawa. He was too stubborn to admit anyone could have misunderstood him. So he lived sixty years in Onawa instead!

Even when we are not dealing with the translation of words from one language to another, as we were in 1945, there are grave misunderstandings in word meanings.

The Process

In fact, someone has said, "Words are in themselves meaningless." They can express ideas or feelings, but they do not possess them. The dictionary recognizes over 14,000 different meanings for only 500 of the most commonly used words. How wrong we can be, if, as listeners, we don't know what meaning the speaker has in mind when using a word!

As our society becomes more conscious of its ethnic groups, the problem of word meanings increases. Chicanos or Blacks or American Indian may be talking in words and terms they, in the inner circle, know and understand very well. They are all speaking English. But if you are not one of them you may be at a total loss to listen to their conversation and understand it.

They, too, have difficulty crossing over ethnic boundaries. A Black may not be able to listen to a Chicano and make sense, and neither may be able to listen understandingly to the American Indian.

They may all be able to repeat every word that was said, but not understand the intra-cultural messages at all!

But an assertive listener in any group will have his ear tuned, like a fine mechanic to the sound of an engine. He will detect possible trouble and avoid a breakdown or interruption in communication.

Good listeners know one thing for sure. Words are not things.

Words Are Not Things

Words are only symbols. They are just an arangement of letters and sounds to put a picture in your mind of something that may be touchable, like a dog, or something that may have no substance at all, like truth, love, or God.

In the case of the last three — truth, love, God — you run a much greater risk, as listener, unless you make sure you know what a person is talking about. These types of words, referring to beliefs, concepts, ideas, and other things you can't see and touch, are what we call "high-order abstracions" and they are very hard to use in conversation because they are very hard to understand. They are the source of much disagreement, anger, frustration, argument, debate, and even war between people, because so few insist on being sure of their meaning to the other fellow.

Listeners have long been put in the role of accepting messages as given because they were afraid to ask what speakers meant when they used words like truth, love, and God.

Next time someone says, "It is the truth!" ask what meaning he or she has assigned to "Truth." See if an explanation you understand can be given.

Words Build Fences Around Ideas

Someday we may invent a thought transfer system to do away with the need for words. When we can project directly an idea from one person to another, without using words in between, we will have eliminated the problems we now encounter.

But that would be a sad day, for in eliminating the magic of words we would have lost a wonderful means of expanding ideas. Words build fences around ideas, but in so doing they do not confine thinking. Rather, they surround and support it.

Assertive listeners will never hold still for a look at an idea completely outside the word fence. They will penetrate that fence to get a clear view of the idea it encases.

Quite often, as in that tragic incident of misunderstanding over "mokumatsu" in 1945, a word ence may be so distorted that it falsifies the intended message. Assertive listeners seek to avoid such tragedies in communication.

The second step in the Assertive Listening process is similar to adjusting the sound on your TV, so you get every word as clearly as possible.

Summary

It is your perfect right, as listener, to make sure you know what the other person is talking about, what meanings are attached to words being used. Assertive Listeners shy away from guessing what is meant. They know it is up to them to get the message straightened out if there is any doubt about it, starting with that slippery item — the WORD.

Assertive listeners deal with words by:
Clarifying the speaker's meaning
Realizing words are merely symbols
Accepting lofty words (truth, love, God) cautiously
Penetrating word fences to get to basic ideas

The Process

**Adjusting the
Picture —
Body and Face
Messages**

We went to a party recently, an alumni reunion, where a couple of young people got pretty annoying.

The girl (we'll call her Gloria) and her boyfriend (we'll call him Bret) were recently graduated from one of our state universities, in the field of psychology. It baffled us at first why they tried to do the things they did.

First, they came into our conversational group abruptly, and started interrupting a line of thought we had found absorbing until they arrived. Then they pushed in closer and closer, nudging us out of the circle.

They were both smoking, dropping ashes without apology. Fortunately, we were on an outside patio and there was no cause for alarm.

Before we backed into the rose bed to wind up full of thorns, their stern faces relaxed and they both looked amused. We were relieved because their change in attitude said something had been going on that we hadn't suspected.

"So you began to feel uncomfortable? You began to think we were pretty obnoxious? We were beginning to move too far into your territory, weren't we?" said Bret.

One of us said, "You bet you were. What's come over you anyhow? When we had you in class you were both models of good communication. Now — all this aggression. . . ."

The Process

Gloria put out her cigarette and moved back a
little. In her old charming manner she said, "Profs,
don't worry. Bret and I were just trying out some of
our new ideas about non-verbal language by ex-
perimenting with aggressive behavior."

"Oh, you mean body language? That popular development of the older science, kinesics?"

"Yes," said Bret, "and the later extension of it
called face language."

"We were just testing you to see how far we could
go before you began to suspect we were acting
out body and facial aggression," Gloria continued.

We, having taught listening all our lives, smiled,
and said, "Well, explain just what you were doing.
We're listening."

"Well, we came into your happy circle, your small
group of college profs, and began breaking up
your line of thought. . . ."

"You certainly did! Then what. . . ."

"Then, we pushed you almost off the patio. . . ."

"Into the rose bed. . . ."

"Then we puffed cigarettes right into your faces,
knowing you are non-smokers, and dropped
ashes on your shoes. . . ."

One of us said, "We had begun to wonder if you had heard about those of us who were born under no-smoking signs. . . ."

"To tell you the truth, we don't smoke either, but we did this time to make a point. . . ."

"Well, verbalize your point. . . .," we said.

"The point we were making," said Gloria, "is that we all need some privacy, some space around us. We usurped all your rights to that privacy. Then we went into an act of body language, pushing and shoving a bit, that spelled outrageous aggression you couldn't understand from us. Then, we looked haughty and blew smoke in your faces, to finally cap the point. We posed a real threat. . . ."

"We challenged you," Bret added, "by using all the aspects of bad body language and face language at once, and we challenged you as listeners to be more assertive. We heard you were writing a book on assertive listening, and wondered if you know how to cope with aggressive non-verbal behavior!"

Well, we all had to laugh. Three lifelong teachers, sold on the idea of assertive listening, caught off-guard and totally incapable of rising to the occasion!

"At least we didn't fight back before we got the message," we said in a rather weak effort at self-defense.

Words aren't the only offenders in message foul-ups, although they can play dirty tricks at times, as we learned in the last chapter. **Acts Speak Louder Than Words**

How people look and act while speaking, how they sit, hold their hands, tilt their heads — all of these can be indicators to skilled listener-observers of what the true message is.

The act that accompanies the words may not seem at all appropriate. A cautious listener will be inclined to give more attention to the body language (non-verbal message) than to the words in this case.

Listening for what has been called "the silent language" by some, is part of an assertive listener's activity. Making judgments about what it means requires a marvelously tuned listening mechanism.

A shrug can mean "So what?" or "I don't know" or "Try it and see" or any number of other things. It is a clue. Nothing more. The skilled listener will take it into account, though, and see what emotion this signal seems to be giving out at this time.

A frown (referring to the area some call "face language") can mean "I disagree" or "I am terribly annoyed" or "I am concentrating on what you say and think while we talk together." The listener in control will not ignore it, and will take into account what it says along with other body language and words. He will understand, too, that the speaker may just have a sudden twinge of charley-horse from sitting in a cramped position.

Listening Through Body Language

The new emphasis on reading body and face language is of major importance to assertive listeners. Although in some cases, body and face communication almost takes over and words are pre-empted or limited to "You know, you know, you know" — "Okay? Okay? Okay?" and the like, we need to be totally aware of the importance of the messages and signals being sent out by movements of the body, and expressions of the face, that fortify or negate oral messages.

The science of non-verbal communication is doing much to explain the pictures given out by the body and face, and learning how to interpret these visual signals will greatly assist you in becoming a skilled and assertive listener.

Listeners find themselves having to listen through body language quite often. As Julius Fast, author of the book, *Body Language,* says, "You've been playing the game of body language unconsciously all of your lifetime. Now start playing it consciously." He promises you will find it "surprising and sometimes a bit frightening," but he also promises it will be "adventurous, revealing and funny."

The Process

The third step in the process of Assertive Listening may be likened to adjusting the picture on your TV set, to clarify what you see.

Summary

Assertive Listeners develop a computer system for incoming messages of all kinds — words, acts, and looks. They are receiving not only verbal messages but those of body and face as well.

The so-called body language and face language message needs to be listened to by means of keen observation and interpretation. The listener must make sure his or her meaning tallies with that of the message giver, and sometimes it means listening through the body language when it takes over completely.

Assertive listeners deal with acts and looks by:

Observing body language carefully

Studying face language cautiously

Interpreting both acts and looks in the spirit with which they are used

Finally, *Combining* verbal (word) and non-verbal (body and face) language to assign meaning to what is heard

The Process

**Judging
The Program**

"That's the last date I'll have with him!"

Margery came in from her third date with Charles to face her roommate, Sue, who couldn't believe her ears.

"Gee, kid, he's so handsome, and he's got lots of money. What happened?"

Margery had been fascinated with Charles at first. He was suave, sophisticated, handsomely dressed. He did seem to have plenty of money. He had taken her to the best places. She had been impressed by his making no demands in return. How could she be so lucky? She, Margery Miller, high school graduate only, secretary, no more than average looking?

Sue was pressing her for an answer. "Hey, wake up, kid. Do you know what you're saying?"

"Yes, I do, Sue," Margery almost snarled. "I am so damn tired of listening to him talk, I could scream. And besides, he just doesn't come on straight."

"What do you mean — 'come on straight'?"

"I mean you never know quite what Charles really means. That's what worries me. The words are OK, he has a great voice, he looks terrific, he holds everyone's attention. But I am not sure at all that what he says is what he means. I can't risk getting in any deeper with him."

It has become an accepted belief in our society that the listener is a receptacle, charged with the responsibility of blandly receiving any message another person sends out.

Facing Up to The Moment of Reckoning

But assertive listeners realize the fallacy of this belief. They know the listener decides on the meaning of the message, after taking into account the meaning of words and of body and face language.

Assertiveness in listening means facing up to the moment of reckoning — passing judgment — after all the facts are in, ALERT to hidden meanings.

Margery was an assertive listener in this respect. The hidden message didn't elude her.

She knew, in her cool, practical evaluation of what Charles had said on three dates and through the way he had said it, that he was not what he might have at first appeared to be. She had the good sense to withhold judgment until she had given him a fair test, as listener. But she also had the good sense to look beyond the surface appearance, the words, the body language, the money! She knew better than to take Charles at face value when she encountered her moment of reckoning with him.

Margery had come from a rather poor farm family. She had learned a great deal about people from practical experience, had worked her way through school and into a good job by applying the common sense approach she had learned at home. She was wary of surface appearances. She had been trained to listen beyond the words, trained to look over the word fences, trained to study the body and face language. She looked for hidden meanings. Though not overly skeptical, she had learned to judge when people were being honest — "coming on straight" — because her parents had often placed great emphasis on this approach to dealing with others.

Having learned the art of being reasonably assertive in getting where she was (pulling herself up by her own bootstraps, as they said in the country), she had also mastered the art of being an assertive listener. She felt perfectly OK about making up her mind about Charles, despite all the surface messages that would lead her astray.

Doing Jury Duty As Listener

Listening might be compared to the jury system. The listener is really the panel of jurors, making judgments, observing, evaluating, and finally making a decision about what has been heard.

An assertive listener realizes his or her activity is important, the final judgmental part of a communication transaction.

In place of twelve men and women listening to evidence, the listener, alone, attends to all the evidence. Often, as in the case of non-stop talkers, the message may run into hundreds and thousands of words, and the open-minded listener may feel like a hung jury at times — believing this, believing that, thrown into a quandary over the final verdict.

When the time comes to make a decision, though, the assertive listener feels equipped to make a good one and feels perfectly justified in arriving at a verdict. He or she feels no sense of guilt in making that decision, even if it's against the person who has been giving the message.

Margery gave up on Charles after listening to him three evenings. She felt justified in deciding, from what she had heard, that he was not giving out good "vibes."

In making the final decision about a message, though, the listener often has to rely on a sixth sense, indefinable, but probably we could come close in meaning if we called it "intuition."

Using The Sixth Sense — Intuition — In Judgments

This intuitive area of judgment comes from experience, practice. It comes from much conscientious listening, and often through trial and error. We know when we put meaning to the message, finally, we have it right, if we bring in this remarkable sixth sense. We know we are in control of the communication transaction.

Margery knew in her own mind that Charles would be a problem. Despite all the messages to the contrary, the looks, money, sophistication, she had that intuitive sense of judgment that gave the truer interpretation of all those desirable-looking aspects of Charles. She saw through, and passed final judgment on, the incoming messages he sent.

Later, when Charles was apprehended for check forgery, it was no big surprise to Margery.

"How in the world did you suspect something was wrong?" Sue asked.

"Well, Sue, I just listened to him, and somehow knew. . . ." said Margery.

Assertive Listening implies putting together the sounds, looks, and other message signals; then, with a sixth sense of intuitive judgment, coming up with an accurate interpretation of what the speaker is really saying.

It is very much like the TV viewer who, having tuned in, cleared up the sound, adjusted the picture to full color, and listened to the total impact, makes a decision to continue listening or to turn off the program. The program is akin to the message. The Assertive Listener, in the final analysis, has the power to keep communication open, or to turn it off.

Summary

The listener assumes the role of jury and feels perfectly justified in rendering a verdict on a message, after taking into consideration all of the input.

Assertive listeners give messages meaning after:

Withholding judgment until all parts of the message are received

Facing up to the moment of reckoning and not relying on wishful thinking

Assuming the role of jury, rendering verdicts fairly after due consideration

Listening to the inner intuitive voice, in testing final judgments

**Reacting and
Acting for Better
Programming**

We were scared stiff.

We were a young family — we Geetings — traveling by station wagon through Mexico with two small sons, and we were terribly lost somewhere between Guanajuato and San Miguel de Allende.

It was the middle of the night, very, very dark. We had only a trail to bump along on. The road had petered out hours ago. Our gas was almost gone. The boys were thirsty and we had no water. It was a moment in life when we didn't know what in the world to do.

Our map, a beautiful official red, white, and blue affair supplied by our U.S. travel agent, had long since been discarded. It simply lied about the short-cut of 79 miles it showed between these two Mexican centers.

Finally, we stopped just before we saw a black hole ahead. Baxter got out and walked a few feet to look into a gaping 70-foot drop, one two-by-four plank laid across it.

We were wary of the Indians nearby. We had seen their campfires flickering in the dark. We feared their machetes and visualized ourselves killed and robbed of all our possessions.

Suddenly, a weathered fierce-looking Indian with long hair and with machete dangling at the waist, appeared from nowhere right beside the car, tapping on the window. He smiled and said, "Lost, Señor?"

Before long, this godly wonderful savior had directed us to a highway of sorts that took us into

---

San Miguel ten minutes later. Baxter showed the map to the manager of the inn, who was wondering what had happened to us and who had a comfortable room waiting.

"Where is the road I see right here on this map?" said Geeting.

"That road," said our genial host after studying the map, ". . . It is, how you say? It is . . . an ASPIRA-TION."

We have never forgotten the feeling of being utterly lost with a perfectly good map in hand.

"The Map Is Not The Territory"

It taught us the lesson assertive listeners very well know — "the map is not the territory." What seems to be a beautiful solution, an ideal way to go in communication, the most workable of democratic processes, may, in fact, be terribly wrong *unless* you have checked, recently, what lies ahead and know what lies behind you.

Also, *unless* you creatively project what might lie ahead (in case things change), you can't rely on any given map. Further, there is always the possibility of having suddenly to change direction completely when all your best guesses are proven wrong.

Still, the assertive listener is more ready than most talkers to chart the way ahead.

How so?

**The Assertive
Listener
Is Aware of
The Main Road**

Skilled listeners know what has gone before, because they have kept track of all the input. They know what road the communication is on, and why the communicators have reached this point in the road.

First, the assertive listener has made few sudden decisions and abrupt judgments. He or she has listened in full color, has not relied on either-or, black-white, acceptance or rejection. The assertive listener does make the decision of listening procedure in any communication, but not until the message has been heard without prejudice, without jumping to conclusions, without opinionated judgments.

Second, the tuned-in listener has been listening for word meanings in the mind of the communicator. Assertive listening means making sure a word being sent is the same as the word being received, and the higher one goes up the abstraction ladder (using words like truth, love, God, etc.) the more determined the listener is to rectify differences in meaning.

Third, the experienced listener is observing body and face language all the time, reading these significant nonverbal signals into the final interpretation of the message. An approving nod may in fact be the total opposite (notice the sneer with it?) or it may be just a relaxing of neck muscles. The assertive listener, competent diagnostician, is not missing any signals and is reading into them the best information available.

Fourth, the good listener has put all of these in-coming signals together and applied an almost sixth sense of intuitive understanding to the real meaning behind the total set of signals. As a jury, he or she has listened to, and compared and evaluated, all the incoming message beacons and arrived at a verdict. Even then, the listener may wish to keep the verdict open for further input.

The assertive listener is fully equipped with background information.

Very often, the one assertive listener in the group is the only one who knows what road the group is on — the main road — and is the only one equip-ped to see ahead.

So, the assertive listener is prepared to chart the way in realizing productive communication.

The Assertive Listener Updates The Map

Instead of sitting complacently while he or she rides along in the back seat of a car on the road to nowhere, facing momentary disaster, the skilled listener is alert at all times, at the driver's wheel, fully informed of the road — behind and ahead. He or she would never be caught off-course in the middle of Mexico on a nonexistent road.

The good listener keeps the map in mind and sees it is updated to include the best information avail-able.

Therefore, the assertive listener, in a communication situation, frequently is the one who sets the course of a group or determines what happens in the case of one-to-one communication.

The listener is completely aware that the talker is almost always speaking from his or her own map — exclusively. All of us have been trained to talk on the basis of our own past experience. In listening, we can readily understand why the speaker is limited in his or her remarks to what is known as a part of his or her background.

Few talkers (although occasionally we find with relief one who breaks the tradition) quote from authorities or give responsible judgments built from wide experience. Instead, they almost always speak from a background limited to myths, prejudice, cherished beliefs, and haphazard notions.

The assertive listener realizes that a large proportion of what passes as communication from the lips of a talker is neatly labeled "GOBBLEDYGOOK."

Assertive listeners try to make a fair judgment of what the speaker's map is based on before agreeing to any part of it.

When the speaker says, "This is the way we must go from here . . .," the active responsible listener will question the background from which the speaker makes such pronouncements. He will study the map the speaker is using, very carefully.

The assertive listener develops the art of being several jumps ahead of the speaker in the communication process. As listener, you will have a pretty good idea of the map as it is shaping up. If others threaten to sidetrack communication, as they often do in meetings, you will be ready to bring the group back to the territory of the main road.

Guiding Communication With Courage

The assertive listener is best equipped to update the map and chart the future course.

In the big roundup of verbal and non-verbal signals from the speaker, the untrained listener is often tempted to sigh, nod approval or acceptance, and give up when the going gets rough, even when the message is obviously full of errors.

It takes exceptional courage to be an assertive listener and assume your responsibility for charting a good map of the territory, for keeping communicators on a main road and getting them to their destination.

Assuming Risk in Charting the Course

Assuming the role of map maker (guide) and all it implies is to take on considerable risk.

How can you be sure the ideas you inject into a meeting to keep communication on course, the meanings you read into speakers' messages, are right?

You can't. It may be that, in your best charted map, you have made an unavoidable error. A hurricane may destroy the road you have charted, or an earthquake rend it to pieces. A flood may cover it with a sudden sheet of water.

Don't feel guilty. You have done your best.

Chances are, however, if you have listened assertively, that you are better prepared than anyone else to chart a productive road for further communication.

In a group, you will have in mind the total agenda of a meeting, for example. You will realize that meetings are horribly misdirected by most chairpersons. In the effort to be very democratic, meetings often are permitted to run on for hours. Final decisions on major areas of concern are often made after three-fourths of the group have gone home and the remaining fourth are tired, mad, drunk, or asleep. An assertive listener can help avoid such a wretched meeting map.

Skilled questioning, neat well-timed motions, soft-spoken words of advice here and there — these might ease many meeting agendas into successful (and far more democratic) pathways. These are the skills of assertive listeners.

If you are a host or hostess, and also an assertive listener, you can construct a successful map for the territory of your party. You can see that guests are brought into the conversation, that they are free from the plague of listening to a monologist who mistakenly sees himself as raconteur. If, indeed, you have the good fortune of entertaining a true raconteur, you will handle interruptions that could throw the party off-track, and help the group get back together in its happy listening mood.

You, assertive listener, are the control agent in most transactions on whatever level. You keep track of where you and others have been, on what main road, and preview the territory ahead. You make the workable map, alert to needed changes as they arise.

You assume the risks, but you chart the course!

Summary

The Assertive Listener, in the end, is the one who, rather like Molly T. in the beginning of this Part I (Process) discussion (first five chapters), makes changes. Although we do not mean to say the listener can tell the speaker what to say, he or she can strongly influence the group reaction to oral messages and often set the course for group action.

Assertive Listeners are the ones who have approached communication situations with an open mind, free of either-or prejudice; have computerized all incoming data, both verbal and non-verbal; have constantly readjusted incoming signals and made basic decisions after careful consideration and the application of a sixth, intuitive sense of fair play — good judgment.

Finally, in mapping or charting the communication, the Assertive Listener constantly reviews the road covered, previews the road as it appears ahead. The Assertive Listener, then, is in the strategic position to guide the total communication process, whether it be on a one-to-one basis or within a group. The listener charts workable maps of a given territory, changes them when need be, and suffers no sense of guilt when, occasionally, the map is wrong.

The Assertive Listener (like a concerned TV viewer) has the power to improve the future — to demand and encourage better programming.

Assertive listeners, finally:

Wait for the whole message, listening in full color

Make good decisions about word meanings, using extreme caution in the area of higher-order abstractions

Make good decisions about non-verbal signals (acts and looks)

Make judgments only after all facts are in and call into play intuitive judgment

Chart the map of the territory

Assume Risks of Error Without Guilt

Part 2

**Expanding
Listening
Know-How**

Skills

**Listening to
Learn**

Skills

We have a friend, a leading chemical engineer in large university, listed in *Who's Who in America,* who said only one word before he was five — "Ahb." It was all he needed to get what he wanted. With a doting grandfather, aunt, and two parents who delighted in supplying his needs, why extend his vocabulary?

When the parents moved from Chicago with Max, the "Ahb" boy, to a small community in Montana, he was thrown with playmates his own age. He soon changed his linguistic habits. In one month, listening to learn by necessity, Max had become almost as fluent as the other little people in the block.

Max, of course, was smart, but it never seemed important to him to learn to talk as long as he didn't need to. Nothing stimulates learning by listening, like necessity.

A personal example proved that to us.

One summer we (Geetings) took a small apartment in Salzburg, Austria, on the old-town side where shopkeepers still expect you to buy your supplies in the language of the country. It didn't take long to master the basics of their special language pattern, although we had spent three years in college German classes to very little avail.

Hunger pangs drove us to listen to learn about how Salzburgers meet, greet, and eat. To learn how they select their foods in a variety of small shops, how they pay for them, and even how they carry them home and store them.

By the third day in residence, we were walking confidently into neighborhood groceries, bakeries, and butcher shops, down to the open-air vegetable and fruit market, carrying our own shopping bags, extending cordial "Gruss Gott" greetings along the way, and thinking of our needs in terms of kilos, grams, and liters while calculating costs in terms of schillings.

Since primitive times listening has been the way people have learned. Beginning in babyhood, humans discover relationships with the world largely through listening. Even totally deaf children "listen" as we think of it in assertive-active terms by observing, touching, and finding other ways of receiving incoming stimuli to compensate for the lack of hearing.

Everyone Learns By Listening

Listening is how the child begins to recognize parents and how parents judge the needs of the child.

When speech begins to develop, it is a mere babble, or vocal play, interrupted by listening. Sound imitation begins for most babies in the sixth month (imitation of their own sounds).

By the time the child is nine months old, it is starting to imitate sounds (though it may not understand them), and to listen with greater satisfaction and discrimination.

By a year and a half, children may use as many as fifty words, often in some kind of sequence that begins to make sense. By thirty months, the child is adding to its vocabulary at a speed surpassing that of any other period in life. By three years, the average child's vocabulary will include more than 1,000 words being used in sentences, much like those heard from older persons.

The deaf child seldom develops speaking ability beyond the babble stage. But, with specific instruction in producing sounds, in using the mouth and tongue to shape words, the deaf child can be taught to speak and be understood.

Listening Loses Out in School

Listening plays a big role in learning in small children. But by the time a child is in the seventh grade learning is transferred mainly to reading — to books. Listening has never been given the academic approval and status accorded to reading. So, the child, from seventh grade on, experiences little focus on the development of listening abilities and is given far more approval for reading efficiency than for listening skill. How many report cards or teachers' evaluations sent home to parents comment on a child's listening improvement?

It's strange that, despite its low status in school, listening continues to be the main way adults learn. If we become dull listeners as we go on in school and arrive at college, is there a course in "Remedial Listening" to equip us for learning on higher levels? There are hundreds of courses in "Remedial Writing" and "Remedial Reading" to ready the non-learner for college life.

Adults Continue to Learn by Listening

Without any real status, then, listening continues to dominate adult life, inexperienced as we become in handling it! In fact, as many studies have shown, nearly half of our communication time is spent in listening. We speak about a third of that time. We read and write the least!

Assertive (controlled, skilled) listening can be the basis for greatly improved business, social, family, or cultural life. If you are going to college or taking instruction of any kind, of course, it is absolutely crucial.

Listening to Learn Is Vital to All Areas of Life

Listening to learn is not passive acceptance of messages of speakers or teachers or doctors or lawyers or anyone else. It is the most assertive part of communication. Remember? A message not received is no message at all.

You, the listener, are of equal importance to the person speaking. You are, in fact, even more important because you are the one who decides how much of the message to accept. And remember, you are the one who clarifies meaning through good questions; you are often the one who makes the message giver stay on the track.

What is the best way to LISTEN TO LEARN, then?

Start by imagining yourself just mastering the skill of driving a car that uses hand gear shifts. Ready?

Getting in Gear

Listening to learn is like getting in the right gear for any road conditions you meet. Get yourself in the proper gear and you are going to be successful under most driving conditions, and most listening conditions.

American gear-shift cars have three or four gears forward. Many experienced drivers would not trade one of these for a power-shift car, because they like being in control and making decisions.

Assertive listeners are like expert drivers, equipped with the built-in skill of knowing what listening gear to shift to for specific situations. They swiftly and easily shift gears as learning conditions change.

Getting in Low Gear to Start (Listening Stimulus Stage)

Usually, you start in low gear, listening carefully to identify problems, if any, and to anticipate what is ahead.

Check your mental attitude for receptivity. Are you excited about learning something new (seeing what's ahead on the road)?

s you open yourself to listen, you are in the
imulus stage. Lots of things start you listening —
e speaker's voice, looks, a good joke. You move
ong cautiously here, getting a comfortable rela-
onship with the speaker, avoiding jamming on
e brakes (if the speaker says something you dis-
ke) or gunning the motor (if the speaker says
omething you like).

hile in low gear, you are noting the stimuli that
art listening — the emotional language, the cool
nemotional approach, the projected outline, etc.
you want to be reinforced for the journey ahead,
ave notepad and pencil in hand to jot down
leas. Sometimes, even, a tape recorder is useful.

low gear you may have to force yourself to go
n listening. A dull opening may tempt you to de-
ide to turn around and go back, to stop listening.
ut wait! Maybe that boring guy is going to show
ou the Grand Canyon just over the hill top. Hang
n there!

f course, as an assertive listener, you are making
e decisions. It is your perfect right to stop listen-
ng if you are sure this is a waste of time. Usually,
nough, the inquisitive mind in search of new ideas
vill keep going, making no snap judgments on the
asis of something not acceptable in the stimulus,
n the opening phase of the communication.

Skills

Shifting to Intermediate Gear, On The Way (Beginning Attention Stage)

Some communication is low gear all the way. If a speaker is talking on a highly technical subject, example, we may have to move so cautiously w never get out of low gear.

Usually, though, once we have ruled out ignorin the speaker or giving up on a subject, and have our attitude adjusted to the thrill of learning some thing new, we shift into a more comfortable mod of reception.

Some American cars have two intermediate shif some only one. As assertive listeners, we develo several intermediate gears. It's good to have at least one intermediate gear for this stage of com munication, where you are between stimulus and unwavering attention.

Intermediate gear is the beginning of the attentic stage.

If we are in a group of people, all talking at once, this is the stage where we focus on one, perhaps to the exclusion of the others.

Studies indicate some persons have the capacit to follow what several people are saying (while in low gear), but we usually zero in on one person who has something of interest to us.

In the case of a platform speaker or teacher, the intermediate gear stage comes when we have found the initial stimulus interesting enough to let us know we want to hear more.

a message is highly technical, again requiring concentrated attention, we proceed in intermediate gear cautiously, refusing to allow our minds to wander. We listen actively, selectively, and critically (yes, we begin to question points in our own minds) and we usually do not miss important points, especially in a learning situation when the subject is presented in a less than effective manner (alas!).

High Gear and Full Speed Ahead (Unwavering Attention Stage)

Some speakers (on stage or in a group) manage to lead us to the freeway very soon after they start talking.

But few are so blessed with the power of intelligent and facile communication.

When we are lucky enough to have such a speaker, we can relax a bit and shift to high gear, gathering ideas like beautiful scenic memories, coming to the end of the journey (as the speaker ends the communication) with a sense of satisfaction in having learned something we won't forget.

Though we infrequently have the pleasure of shifting into high gear, we still have a problem getting the maximum out of a learning experience as we listen unless we remember some important things about the mental process and how it functions while listening.

So, let's consider how you can always stay within the speed limits, even in high gear.

Skills

Proceeding Within the Speed Limits

While it might seem that, once we encounter a highly entertaining speaker, we have nothing to prevent total relaxation and top speed, our mental processes have a way of getting out of control. There are good reasons to keep within speed limits in order to arrive safely and avoid problems, as we listen.

The mind is always ahead of the speaker. You, as listener, are way out ahead. You can think circles around the speaker because even a fast talker can't keep up with your capacity to receive messages. And the mind is a bad child unless kept under control.

Most Americans talk about 135 words a minute, which is a dead stall for some minds and sluggish even for the average brain that can receive words at rates from 400 to 800 per minute.

So, what do you do with your free listening time?

If you're just an average, non-assertive listener, you'll turn on and off, figuring you can always get back on the road. But, if you're an assertive listener, you'll use your spare listening time to think ahead to what might be coming (where is the speaker taking me?) and to think back (where have we been?). You will constantly scrutinize the points being made to see if they have good support evidence. You won't just take ideas on faith. You will observe the body and face language, to see if something contrary to the speaker's words is being signaled.

onstantly, even in high gear, the assertive lis-
ener remains very active. As such a listener you
eep on the alert for sudden interruptions,
witches, sidetracking of ideas. You get all the
eaning there is — verbal, non-verbal, overt, and
idden — from the message.

would be great if the mind could act like a tape
corder. A few do, but not many of us are blessed
ith total recall. We have to depend on memory
ut it isn't always reliable. Still, as assertive listen-
rs we will have at our command all of the best
own and proven ways of recalling what we
ant, of things heard.

**Banking What
You Have Heard**

ow do we prevent things from going in one ear
nd out the other?

Skills

There are reliable techniques to bank in our memory quite a bit of what we would recall.

We are all limited, of course, by what we already know from reading, from listening, from experience. This already banked knowledge is called our "frame of reference." Almost everything we take in is understood in terms of what we already know.

But much of what we remember is what we want remember. Our psychological needs, sense of values, beliefs, prejudices, and hopes color our listening retention. Maybe someone said twenty-five years ago that you looked handsome one evening. Did you ever forget it? No! You can still recall the exact time, exact place, exact words. Because you want to, that's why!

Memory of things heard, seen, or experienced, in both pictures and words, and in some cases memory storage of emotions, are part of everyone's equipment. But we can't always bank on it! Sometimes it is nearly impossible to recall what you desperately want to recall.

How do we bring things out of memory storage?

We all have short-term and long-term memory banks. In one (short-term) we toss telephone numbers, grocery lists, and names of people we've just met at a party and never expect to see again. In the other (long-term) we store, with the hope we can recall them as needed, ideas and facts and experiences that have lasting meaning to us.

Association with something already in the long-term bank helps. As you listen, when an idea is presented that you desperately want to re-member, search your bank for an association with something already a permanent part of you.

Limiting the number of things you want to re-member also helps. As you listen, try to feed your bank account the most significant ideas and rein-force them with some association. Don't expect your mind to remember all the points. A good speaker will, of course, take some responsibility for you, and limit the number of points he or she makes, and keep reinforcing them. But not too many speakers are so skilled. So, it is up to you to decide on the number of points you can re-member and then associate them with what you already have in your memory storage.

Listening banking should go on long after a speech or a conversation or some other experi-ence has given you a memorable item.

Keeping an Active Bank Account

In assertive listening, you have been quite dis-criminating in selecting certain ideas to re-member. Later you may want to think over these ideas in private or discuss them with someone else to weigh your own reactions and reinforce your memory.

Judgment and evaluation of what is listened to are part of the assertive listening process. You, of course, are the only judge qualified to know what belongs in your memory bank, and you don't have to clutter it up with a lot of facts and ideas, meaningless to you.

In order to complete the listening-to-learn process, analysis and judgment of what has been taken in should occur regularly. Keep your bank account active. Discard the useless. Reinforce the useful.

Time may change your views about what to keep, what to discard, of course. Knowing more about a speaker may give you respect for what he or she has to say, even though on first hearing you judged that speaker a loss.

And time, itself, changes ideas and facts.

In college, we (Geetings) had a splendid Professor of Astronomy, a woman, judged by us the best prof on the campus. She predicted, in no uncertain terms because she knew it to be a fact, that man would never get to the moon. Her support evidence was conclusive. Man, if he started at birth, could not live long enough to get there, even traveling 200 miles an hour, and he couldn't breathe in outer space.

But look at what has happened since the dear woman's death!

We have, in our own memory bank, a vivid picture of our dear prof giving us the truth about outer space travel. But we have had to scrap that so-called "truth."

Summary

Since primitive times listening has been a major way people have learned. The baby learns much through listening, including how to talk. Children continue to learn by listening until about the seventh grade, when reading takes precedence. From there on, listening is given a minor role in education.

Assertive Listening to learn is crucial in many areas — business, social, family, educational, and cultural life. It can be compared to driving a gear-shift car in which the driver (listener) has full control, going from gear to gear as the road conditions (situations) require. The stages of listening to learn may be compared to Low Gear (Stimulus Stage), Intermediate Gear (Beginning Attention Stage), and High Gear (Unwavering Attention Stage).

Listening to learn requires the listener to make use of the free time he or she has (the lapse between mental processes and time to deliver the spoken message). Spare time should be used to think ahead, think back to what has been said, to examine points being made, and to observe non-verbal language.

Finally, listening to learn ends with storage in the Long-Term Memory Bank of desired information, ideas, etc. This is accomplished by finding a link within one's already existing "frame of reference," limiting the number of items to be stored, and then judging and reviewing periodically what is banked.

Assertive listening to learn means:

Finding the appropriate mode to suit the listening situation (like shifting to the right gear for road conditions when driving)

Developing the ability to shift gears as needed

Making use of free time experienced during listening intake

Storing in long-term memory bank what listener wants to retain

Judging and reviewing contents of memory bank

**Analytical
Listening**

There comes a time in all of our lives when we must listen with caution, care, reason. Some listening specialists have called this critical listening, but we resist that term because it brings to mind false notions about what we really mean. "Critical" so often means finding fault and showing disapproval. What we are discussing does not necessarily mean that, although we can't rule out finding flaws, faults, and lies in another person's message, through listening.

What we wish to discuss here is in-depth listening. Probing listening. Uncovering-the-facts listening. Projecting-what-they-might-mean listening. For want of a better term, we will call all of this Analytical Listening.

But here is a story to illustrate what we mean:

One of the biggest food chains in the United States decided some years back to announce a policy of "meeting all competition in pricing."

Customers were urged to check all items on the shelves and, if they could find any of them being sold for less in another store, they were asked to bring this information to the attention of the chain's local manager. They were guaranteed a matching, or lower, price.

This rash decision came about in this way, according to one of our students who was working in the administrative offices of the food chain at the time.

The national manager of the chain summoned top administrators and announced a policy he had decided would bring the chain to public attention immediately. It was "match all prices," no matter how low. The five or six administrators present a-greed this would be a great way to get lots of new customers.

One lonely administrative assistant (the student), who happened to be in the room, had immediate second thoughts. But he knew his place. At that time, the hierarchy didn't entertain ideas from those under the top-top level. The assistant feared speaking up.

But on the way back to the office, he said to his boss: "Have we considered what might happen as a result of this policy? In analyzing what I heard, I tend to project a ganging up of competing stores. What is to prevent them from giving the public a wide assortment of 'loss leaders' and running our chain right out of business?"

His boss looked shocked for a moment. But he told the young assistant he'd better keep his doubts to himself. Time would tell.

And it did. Before long, the food chain was feeling the repercussions of its benevolent-sounding pol-icy. Managers across the nation were distraught as they had to mark, below cost, one item after the other. The cumulative effect of these below-cost items was proving disastrous. Needless to say, the policy of "meeting all competition" had to be discontinued with some loss of face.

As the student reported in class, when we were discussing analytical listening, this episode taught him a lesson. Never take "on faith" what you hear, even though in the process you must, as a good assertive listener, remain openminded, avoid judgmental reactions, and withhold negative response until you have heard a person out.

Nobody expects you, as an assertive listener, to be a fool.

If you discover, through a process of careful analytical listening, that something is wrong, or is going wrong, you have a perfect right and a responsibility to speak up. Assertive listeners are not denied the privilege of being assertive talkers too.

Had my student, as the young assistant, spoken up at the time the food chain was initiating the "meet all prices" policy, the problems it encountered might have been effectively avoided. On the other hand, he might have lost his job!

What Is Analytical Listening?

We have already suggested what we mean by this term, analytical.

Let us consider it a bit further in relation to other listening skills we are discussing in this book. It is NOT:

Listening emotionally to friends, lovers, and family. (TLC listening is better suited to this.)

Listening to college lectures and major speakers. (Listening for information is the skill best used here.)

Listening to all kinds of things, like music, wind, ideas, etc., etc., to invent or create something new. (Creative listening will help here.)

However, analytical listening can, and should, be a part of all of these other listening skills. Keeping analytical listening skills in mind as you use any of the other types of listening will greatly augment and reinforce your listening dimensions, and will help you come to better decisions.

In general, here are the qualities that distinguish analytical listening: It is listening in low gear. Listening very cautiously and carefully. Listening for basic truth (so far as it can be ascertained). Listening to reveal attractively packaged lies. It is, in reality, separating the chaff from the wheat, opinion or prejudice from fact. It is sleuthing out the "hidden persuaders."

We are used to the warning: LET THE BUYER BEWARE.

Let's add another worth remembering: LET THE LISTENER EVALUATE.

Unfortunately, all kinds of undesirable things occur in the absence of evaluative, analytical listening. Such as.

What Happens Without Analytical Listening?

Families disintegrate and children run away from home.

Politicians promise things they can't produce and the public loses respect for politics and government.

College professors turn into bores and collegians give up coming to class.

We could make a list of a thousand items. The world's ills are allowed to develop and multiply because so few of us are assertive listeners. We may be highly intelligent, read the papers every day, and listen to the best programs on television, but we remain apathetic, listless listeners, unresponsive, unconcerned about incoming stimuli.

History is full of the tragedies resulting from passive listening.

Look to the victimization by Hitler of one of the best educated, most industrious, and intelligent peoples on earth. Had they listened analytically, they would have discriminated between realism and fantasy. Some did, of course, and got out of Germany.

Recently, in our own country, we witnessed a fiasco of mammoth proportions in the White House, because so few analytical listeners were evaluating such statements (for hidden truth) as: "We have had no spy planes flying over Russia" (we learned, subsequently, that we had); "I will not resign" (but the then Vice-President did resign); and "I'm not a crook!" (comment not necessary).

Without asserting ourselves to listen analytically, we get to accepting gossip and rumor because it gives us a secret thrill to uncover something about someone we didn't suspect (though later proved untrue). Often we fail to question the basis of inferred slander.

We are subjected to constant persuasion. TV commercials tell us which foods will solve breakfast problems without exertion, which deodorants will keep us smelling good, which aspirin will do better than others in easing a headache.

Fortunately, cigarette advertising has been removed from our listening life, although it continues to support many magazines and newspapers. But, we have been far better trained in analytical reading than in analytical listening.

The listener in control of his own responses, the assertive listener, is always conscious of the special skills needed when analytical listening is required.

What Happens With Analytical Listening?

As in almost all listening, he or she neither accepts nor rejects the speaker's comments without knowing for sure what is in the speaker's mind. To clarify the speaker's points, the assertive listener will probe with questions such as: "What do you mean by that?" or "Explain more precisely your point of view." Often, the assertive listener will restate the points made to see if they agree with what the speaker had in mind. "Let me see if I can restate what you just said. . . ."

But, beyond the general approach to assertive listening, there are a couple of very important things to remember in the case of analytical listening.

They are these:

First, in analytical listening, it is most essential that one consider the integrity of the source.

Second, it is equally important that one weigh the evidence for two things — its timeliness and its completeness.

Let us consider these further:

**Evaluating
The Source of
Evidence**

Most of us have learned to make an effort to judge the integrity of people who try to persuade us to BUY someting, DO something, or BELIEVE IN something.

In other words, we take the preacher's word for what we should believe in over the car salesman's word. But the car salesman is a better authority, in most cases, on what a certain car can do and why it might be a good buy.

If we are being persuaded to BUY a car, home, stocks or bonds, etc., we consider the credentials (or background) of the salesperson. Too much old-time pressure may cloud all the points the salesperson is making. High-pressure salesmanship is going out of style. More modern techniques of salesmanship have developed because people, fortunately, are getting more sensitive and selective in listening to sales pitches. Analytical listeners, even a few, are beginning to demand that salespersons have a reputation for honesty and integrity, just as anyone else in business must have.

If we are being persuaded to DO something like vote for a woman instead of a man, switch from Republican to Democrat, or shed thirty pounds to avoid a heart attack, we usually check out the credentials of the person talking to us. Analytical listeners seldom get swept into making basic changes, doing something foreign to their life-styles. They look to the competency of the persuader first.

Finally, if we are being urged to BELIEVE IN something such as a religious creed, we consider the background of the persuader — the preacher, evangelist, priest, rabbi, guru, etc. We may assume such persons are fully informed and prepared to give us expert direction and sound advice, but analytical listeners seldom rely on such assumptions. They take very little "on faith" alone.

Analytical listeners learn to distinguish between skepticism and blind acceptance. There is a whole world of choice between these two polar opposites.

Generally, trained assertive listeners do believe in the basic goodness of civilization, however. They tend to agree with Kenneth Clark, who notes in his splendid book, *Civilisation,* "It is a lack of confidence more than anything else, that kills a civilisation. We can destroy ourselves by cynicism . . . just as effectively as by bombs."

The analytical listener will avoid disillusionment about those who try to persuade him to BUY, DO, or BELIEVE IN something, by realistically assessing their qualifications to act as persuaders.

Weighing The Evidence For Timeliness and Completeness

Currently, we are deluged with arguments pro and con on the subject of nuclear power. Some inform us of its advantages. Others, of its disadvantages. If we lack the capacity for analytical listening, we risk being swept into the ranks of those who firmly believe nuclear plants are a hazard or into the opposing ranks of those who believe they are absolutely safe.

But that, we find through careful, cautious, in-depth listening, is hardly the question — "at this point in time."

Richard E. Tuttle, a member of the California State Energy Resources Conservation and Development Commission, makes this clear in a carefully developed article in which he says: "The issue (now) is not nuclear safety . . . any answers will necessarily be tentative, subject to change, perhaps on rather short notice. . . . in areas of advancing science and technology today's 'correct' answer may be incorrect by tomorrow. . . ."

uttle urges a careful investigation of the total problem of supplying energy (all probable sources) and reminds us that in this area "disputes among small nations on the other side of the earth may suddenly cut off fuel supplies."

Finally, he wisely advises, "Where there are no permanent answers, the only predictable constant is the need for flexibility, and the capacity to respond to changed conditions. . . ."

Timeliness of evidence is crucial in a society changing as rapidly as ours. Relying on the facts of specialists who did research over ten years ago may carry considerable risk. Government statistics, scientific evidence, and even religious verities, are subject to change with our changing times.

Analytical listeners check all evidence for its dateline.

In addition, analytical listeners evaluate the completeness of information being given in support of a point of view, knowing that one set of statistics is no certain proof, one quoted authority is hardly sufficient to support a point.

Imagine accepting a real estate salesperson's evaluation of your property without checking out all the values around you!

Imagine taking a college professor's words without question, if you know he or she is lecturing from notes written down five, ten, or fifteen years ago! Notes primarily from one or two sources!

Imagine swallowing enormous amounts of vitamin C without checking more than one man's word that it will do wonders warding off and correcting colds!

Do you check all evidence for timeliness and completeness? If not, you have work to do on your skills as an analytical listener.

Remaining in Control of The Situation And Yourself

It's hard not to listen sometimes with a chip on the shoulder.

It's especially hard to listen to someone with limited information, reinforced by narrowminded prejudice.

You are tempted to walk away looking disgusted. Or to shout back something like, "You're nuts, you know that?" Or do something even worse that you'll regret later, because these reactions come from a basic childishness and lack of control. Being assertive as a person, as a listener, doesn't give anyone the privilege of being socially obnoxious.

The analytical listener looks for errors of statement, doubtful inferences, insufficient or out-of-date evidence, but not with a vengeance. First of all, the analytical listener is assertively openminded. Even when a speaker has an axe to grind, the listener gives him a chance before passing judgment.

But the analytical listener reserves the privilege of refusing to blindly accept opinions without support or timeliness.

The assertive listener is conscious of his or her own biases too. Self-evaluation is honestly faced. If I was brought up Catholic or Republican or pro-Women's Lib, I must take that into consideration in evaluating my reactions to what I hear. I realize I hear differently, understand differently, than I would had I been reared Jewish or Democrat or anti-Women's Lib. But I will make allowances for my own prejudices and try to be realistically fair in judgment.

The analytical listener is aware of internal inconsistencies and shortcomings.

Self-examination requires objective self-awareness. It demands a basic honesty that few in our society have. It means we are prepared to realize, as Caesar once did, that "the fault, dear Brutus, is not in our stars, But in ourselves. . . ."

Analytical listening takes great self-respect and self-control which only the trained assertive listener is apt to have. It means remaining in command of the communicative situation — and of yourself.

Skills

Summary

Analytical Listening means listening with caution, care, and reason; listening critically in the best sense of the word. It is in-depth listening and is useful in all other types of listening (TLC listening, listening for information, and listening creatively).

Qualities which distinguish Analytical Listening include listening in low gear, cautiously and carefully, for basic truth, and separating fact from preju diced opinion.

National disasters of all kinds and personal tragedies result from imperfect listening, but Analytical Listening helps to ferret out lies and "hidden persuaders" and other ills of society.

In Analytical Listening, a person seeks to clarify obscure points through careful questioning, judge the integrity of sources, and weigh the evidence for timeliness and completeness. Finally, the listener checks his or her own biases, inner inconsistencies, and prejudicial background influences. Through it all, the assertive listener remains in control of the communication and the self.

Analytical listening means:

Following good listening techniques already described, such as remaining openminded, withholding judgment, etc.

Clarifying, through questioning, any obscure points

Questioning sources for integrity and reliability

Questioning The Timeliness and Completeness of data offered in terms of persuasion

Throughout, *Remaining in control of communication and one's self*

**Listening to Help
(TLC Listening)**

More important than food, more vital than rest, almost more crucial than shelter, is the overwhelming human need for TLC (Tender Loving Care), a large share of which is related to listening.

TLC Listening is at the heart of many social efforts to solve the crying needs of humans. For example, Suicide Prevention, Alcoholics Anonymous, Weight Watchers, and other groups emphasize the necessity of one-to-one relationships in which TLC Listening is of major importance.

A sympathetic ear, especially a trained sympathetic ear, is often the life saved, the needed medicine, the precise therapy for a particular problem.

But we all need TLC Listening to stay stable, to overcome distress, to remain active and alert. This need begins in infancy, as we shall see.

Babies Demand TLC Listening

A number of studies of children who have been denied TLC, with its Listening component, reveal shocking facts.

For example, one study by Dr. Rene A. Spitz, highly respected in the field of psychoanalytic research, followed the lives of 91 babies in a foundling home outside the United States.

These children had been with their mothers during the first three to four months, showing normal development, but were then separated from them and sent to a foundling home. Here, one nurse had to care for eight to twelve little ones. The babies soon showed the ravages of "emotional starvation," often referred to as "marasmus" or "withering away."

Their physical development was greatly retarded. Their faces became vacuous and some of them began to take on the look of imbeciles. They indulged in bizarre finger movements. By the age of four, some of them had not learned to sit, stand, walk, or talk. Dr. Spitz reports that "a distressingly high percentage of these children" suffered "marasmus."

Of the original 91, well over one-third (37%) had died within two years.

By comparison, in another nursery where children were cared for by their mothers, "not a single death occurred among 220 children observed during a four-year period."

Dr. Spitz concludes: "It appears that emotional starvation leads to progressive deterioration. . . ."

All Humans Need TLC Listening

Emotional starvation, as we conceive it in relation to listening, sets in when we lack human, intimate contacts that give us an opportunity to be heard.

Think of that the next time you see anyone, any age, any sex, who is despondent, passive, unhappy, ill, frenzied, withdrawn, or aggressive. The direction Listening "marasmus" can take is varied.

How many "winos" on skid rows throughout the world could have been saved by TLC Listening?

How many of those thousands of teenagers who run away from home each year to take up some distressing lifestyle could have been restored to health by TLC Listening?

How many of those acquaintances you avoid inviting to dinner, because you fear their non-stop talking will ruin the party, could be encouraged to restore a sense of balance in communication if anyone ever took the time to give them what they so desperately need, TLC Listening?

How many business administrators could solve their problems at once by turning their attention to TLC Listening to subordinates, knowing that such an effort is not weak? TLC Listening takes control, demands courage, threatens risk, is certainly not for the timid.

"Getting command of the situation" often means assertively drawing on one's skills of TLC Listening.

TLC Listening vs. "Egocentric Power Over Other People"

Dr. Rollo May, eminent psychologist and bestselling author, emphasizes the necessity for facing up to radical changes in our society that call for "the capacity to move ahead in spite of despair. . . ."

He calls this an "assertion of self, a commitment." And he speaks of a new type of courage demanded by this commitment. Ruling out "egocentric power over other people" as a courageous act, Dr. May proposes instead "a new form of courage . . . the use of the body for the cultivation of sensitivity. . . . This will mean the development of the capacity to listen with the body . . . as the means of empathy with others. . . ."

The belief that power is achieved through intimidation of others is popular in this society. Examples of realizing success, increasing monetary income, and fulfilling the need to be some kind of hero or heroine have been filling pages of best-sellers.

But TLC Listening, used assertively by a person who understands the process involved, the skills, the risks, and the hoped-for outcome, is something far apart from intimidation.

The principal motive in TLC Listening is to bring the other person into a position of equality, into a position where he or she feels OK. As explained in the popular book on Transactional Analysis, the desired-for life position underlying people's behavior is the *I'm OK – You're OK* (at peace with each other, at peace with oneself, communicating on the adult level) position. At such a level, people no longer have to play games with each other, and can come on "perfectly straight" in their communication.

TLC Listening and Intimacy

As vital as touch may be in Tender Loving Care, there are times when it is impractical and presence alone can weld personalities together in a stable relationship.

Coleridge and Wordsworth, two English poets, could spend an evening sitting before an open fireplace, hardly exchanging a word, yet their diaries note the warmth of feeling and the memory of a fascinating conversation.

We may have sat beside a loved one who was very ill. Words may have been few, but there was a strong sense of intimacy that resulted just from being together.

At times, the greatest help we can give another, and certainly the strongest bond of intimacy we can offer, is the willingness to listen to that person talk through his or her ideas, hopes, dreams, plans, or — quite often — failures.

Building healthy relationships in the family depends on much TLC Listening. True intimacy cannot be attained on the strictly physical level; it demands more of us than that. As Rollo May has said, "It is easier in our society to be naked physically than to be naked psychologically or spiritually — easier to share our body than to share our fantasies, hopes, fears, and aspirations." These are more personal, and exposing them to others makes us vulnerable to criticism. So, some very unhappy people, indulgent and promiscuous in sexual relationships, are exposing their great inner need for a type of intimacy that eludes them when they have no TLC Listener with whom to share their innermost thoughts.

TLC Listening is fundamental in every relationship where "authentic intimacy" is crucial. By authentic, we mean genuine, real, as opposed to superficial and artificial.

When the parent gives the child TLC Listening, the child will expand and grow. When the parent ignores this human need, the child will often go elsewhere to find help, or will become reclused. Or, the child may become frenetic in an effort to be listened to, and develop into a "problem child."

When the husband listens with TLC to the wife, there is a sense of intimacy and concern for the marriage not found in less equalitarian relationships. The woman's movement has opened the eyes of society to the great need many women have to be listened to after a long day at home with the children. Whereas it has been traditional in our society for the woman to be prepared to handle the husband's problems at the end of a long day at the office, researchers of "secret alcoholism" among women have found that the need of wives and mothers for TLC Listening is probably greater than that of tired-of-the-office husbands.

Close marriages and love relationships are always built on TLC Listening on the part of both partners. Anything less leads to secret resentment, frustration, and faked intimacy on the part of the cheated partner.

To listen with concern in social and business relationships does not imply a maudlin, sentimental approach. Such would be far from "authentic intimacy." It merely implies a listening stance relatively free of judgment, interruption, and condemnation. It also implies a listening attitude that is calm, attentive, and understanding.

To practice TLC Listening, you must have worked out your own hostilities and calmed your own anxieties. TLC Listening is a job for those in control, first of all of themselves!

How to Listen With Tender Loving Care

The skills of TLC Listening are built on the process of Assertive Listening as explained in Part I of this book. But, in the case of TLC, the listener will be placing more emphasis on certain aspects of the process — particularly on the willingness to withhold reaction, especially negative, and hear the other person to completion.

Dr. Carl Rogers, well known in the field of counseling through listening, has found that patience in the listening process cannot be overestimated. He identifies this type of listening, however, as "active," and as a process in which the listener does not "passively absorb the words which are spoken to him." Rather, he actively tries to grasp facts, feelings, and attitudes in what he hears and, through listening, help the speaker work out his or her own problems. With the aid of the trained listener, the troubled person thus becomes his or her own therapist.

Most of us would not want to think of ourselves as psychiatrists trained in therapeutic skills, nor would we want to assume the responsibility for healing of deep-seated ills that paid professionals handle.

But that is no reason to avoid practicing TLC Listening, which is, in some respects, related to the type of listening psychiatrists must do.

open a TLC Listening session, it is well to try to
d a suitable place and time. It is very hard to
ake much of a success of this type of listening
a crowded subway, holding on to an overhead
ap, and knocking into your neighbor. Much bet-
, if possible, that you start listening before a
arm fireplace, with no danger of phones inter-
oting or pots boiling over on the stove!

ur attitude, as listener, should be hopeful. As an
sertive listener, you already know you are in
ntrol of the situation and can handle what de-
lops with appropriate reaction and direction.

e receiving stage is crucial. The troubled per-
n may vary depending on circumstances and
periences. His or her ego is at stake. If this per-
n senses you are going to play God or give a
rmon or even interrupt with a raised eyebrow,
at may be the end of this session of TLC Listen-
g.

ontinuing with an attitude of acceptance, non-
reatening in your behavior, you will encourage
e speaker to move to an honest appraisal of his
her problem. Being too casual, on the other
and, you may give the feeling that you don't really
are. A thoughtful balance between concern and
onchalance is called for and indicated in how
ou look at the person and react to what is said.
enerally, a kind, steady, eye-to-eye contact ac-
ompanied with occasional nods of understand-
g will encourage the other person to speak
eely.

Your task is not to counsel. It is to let the other person — husband, wife, child, lover, business associate, friend — speak freely without interruption. An occasional word of acknowledgment that the message is getting through is OK. Response not outlawed. Show that you are interested and willing to listen on.

Occasionally, you may wish to test your understanding of the other person: "Did I understand you to say. . . .?"

As a result of the listening session, the other person may ask for your opinion.

This is a challenge you must meet with the best resources at your disposal. Usually, however, the person does not need rules and regulations, guidelines, recitals of "thou shalt nots," etc., from you. If you have done your proper TLC Listening most fairly normal persons will have talked themselves into reasonable decisions about what they should do as a result of their problems. Most people work themselves out of their own quandaries, with the help of an experienced, assertive listener, equipped to do TLC Listening.

The Rewards of TLC Listening

In addition to the obvious help you can give to someone else in providing a TLC Listener, you will benefit in many ways.

Naturally, an improved communication with those with whom you want to be close — spouse, business associate, friend, is a major reward. The enrichment from communication at an authentically intimate level is of benefit to both parties.

98

metimes, through regular sessions of TLC Lis-
ning, we can change a bad situation, such as a
umbling marriage, into a good one. A husband's
tening to an overburdened "homemaker" has
en known to restore her equilibrium and take
vay her obsession with alcohol. The wise hus-
and, in this case, is the winner in that he regains
happy marriage.

stening to employees has brought about a
engthening of their relationship to the company,
d the employer who practiced TLC Listening
on their respect and loyalty.

Carl Rogers has pointed out, also, persons who
actice sensitive listening "tend to listen to them-
lves with more care" and are able to make
hers understand better how they feel and think.
Not the least important result of listening is the
ange that takes place within the listener himself.
esides providing more information than any other
ctivity, listening builds deep, positive relation-
ips and tends to alter constructively the at-
udes of the listener," says Rogers.

ne of the great rewards of getting to know others
hrough TLC Listening) is that you end up know-
g a lot more about yourself.

hrough listening to nurture others, you win self-
ontrol, self-awareness, and self-respect. What
reater rewards could you possibly seek than
ese?

Skills

Summary

Tender Loving Care, "authentic intimacy," is an overwhelming human need from infancy to old age. A large share of this need is dependent on listening, TLC Listening.

Emotional starvation leads to basic problems of despondency, passivity, illness, withdrawal, and even aggressive behavior. Correction of the underlying problems resulting in such behavior ma rest with the assertive listener who knows how to call on his or her skills as a TLC Listener when needed.

TLC Listening is the opposite of attaining "egoce tric power over other people." It is the assertion c self to listen as a means of empathy with others, t help them.

TLC Listening rewards the listener, however, with improved communication in all areas. Winning friends by benefiting them, winning better business relations by listening to employer or employee problems, are just examples of rewards to be gained by the practitioner of TLC Listening.

Skills in general are similar to those outlined in Pa I, with a heavier-than-usual emphasis on withhold ing judgment, observing non-verbal behavior, and patience to listen to completion.

Assertive TLC listeners do the following:
Respect the crucial need to give TLC listening opportunities to others — children, business associates, friends, and enemies

---

Always resist exerting "Egocentric power over other people" — that is, guard against intimidating others in favor of encouraging them to solve their own problems through TLC Listening

Use TLC Listening in "authentic intimacy" — they do not fake interest, they give real interest and concern, they build confidence in the troubled person and strive to have him or her feel perfectly OK, on a level of equality

Practice basic skills of good listening with added emphasis on patience to hear the message to completion without judgment, interruption, or condemnation.

**Creative
Listening**

What would you do if someone told you to do nothing but listen?

Could you turn your listening into a great painting
An opera? A Broadway hit? A TV special?

Creative listeners have done all of these things —
have received through their ears the substance fc
prize-winning works of art, memorable plays, anc
great books.

**Listening as a
Creative Force**

Walt Whitman, beloved nineteenth century poet,
fashioned one of his most memorable works
around listening.

In his poem called *Song of Myself,* Whitman
clearly demonstrated the difference between
common and uncommon, lethargic and creative,
listening.

"Now I will do nothing but listen," he began, and
    then he told us why.

"Now I will do nothing but listen,

To accrue what I hear into this song, to let sounds
    contribute toward it,

I hear bravuras of birds, bustle of growing wheat,
    gossip of flames, clack of sticks cooking my
    meals.

I hear the sound I love, the sound of the human
    voice,

I hear all sounds running together, combined,
    fused or following.

Sounds of the city and sounds out of the city,
    sounds of the day and night. . . ."

Whitman goes on, in his wide-ranging emotional empathy to sounds, to recall the laughter of workers, the "faint tones of the sick," the voice of the judge pronouncing a death sentence. He remembers the sounds of alarm-bells, steam whistles, and trains. On another aesthetic level he relistens to the violoncello, "the Key'd cornet" that "shakes mad-sweet pangs through my belly and breast." He recalls the chorus, the tenor and soprano of grand opera, the orchestra that "whirls me wider than Uranus flies."

And, in the end, breathless with the excitement of remembered sounds, Whitman feels "the puzzle of puzzles . . . that we call Being."

Listening, to Whitman, was a creative force, as it has been to many poets and writers as well as artists of all categories.

But listening as a creative force touches the common man and woman as well, if they are tuned in. Even in everyday encounters.

Brenda Ueland, in an article that once appeared in *The Ladies Home Journal,* explained this when she said, "When we listen to people there is an alternating current, and this recharges us so that we never get tired of each other. We are constantly re-created . . . this expressing and expanding . . . makes the little creative fountain inside us begin to spring and cast up new thoughts and unexpected laughter and wisdom."

Creative listening, with its potential for recreating those around us and ourselves, is a skill almost anyone can master. It is not reserved for the privileged few who now practice it. Learning to listen creatively is one of the rewards of those who conscientiously master the full range of possibilities within assertive (controlled) listening.

Who Are The Creative People? Creative people are sometimes insane, but not always. Salvador Dali, the artist of startling surrealism, explains, "The only difference between a madman and myself is that I am not mad." Van Gogh was distraught and, in a moment of insanity, cut off his ear, as we are often reminded, but we can't blame his creativity for that. Among outstanding artists we have hundreds of stable, well-balanced people.

Creative people are those who arrive at something new.

Their numbers are limited, not so much by a slighting of talent in people as because of a lack of respect for creativity in our society. Creativity doesn't always bring you money or fame. It is not always given a chance to flourish, and one place where it is usually ruled out early in the maturation process is at school.

About the only elementary class in which creativity is considered the teacher's business is the art class (and there are fewer and fewer of these as budgets tighten.) Here, however, we find such common barriers to creative development as those terrible, restrictive coloring books and pattern workbooks — worse than nothing!

Edisons, Marconis, and Einsteins are not motivated through early exposure to "creative experiences" like coloring books, but they might be encouraged with a multitude of truly motivating experiences — fine films, field trips, good materials
with which to make things. There is considerable
support for the idea that a child introduced to
creative thinking in an art class can transfer the
creative approach to classes in science, even
math!

Great scientists are basically creative in approach
— searching for the new. So are the Picassos,
Beethovens, and Shakespeares.

Creative people are around in all fields of en-
deavor: science, engineering, mathematics, business, industry, the arts, and homemaking. They
are creative because they somehow have learned
to make use of their senses of sight, touch, smell,
taste, and hearing in perceiving the world with a
difference that makes a difference.

Creative people are more assertive in the use of
their senses (and in exploring what they learn
through them) in combinations that produce
something new. A creative cook can be going
through a process similar to that of a creative artist. They both come up with novel and uncommon
use of materials, unusual solutions to problems,
uncommon answers to common questions. New
ideas spring from their minds often in response to

How Does I.Q. Relate to Creativity?

something they have heard. It may be the same sound or sounds thousands of others have also heard but passed over with no reaction or experimentation.

How does creativity differ from I.Q. (intelligence quotient)?

Why are some very smart people so rigid?

How come some people with marvelous memories are in low-paying jobs?

We can measure I.Q. somewhat, but valid tests for creativity are still not available. Authorities say that, of the 28 dimensions of the mind needed for major scientific discovery, a creative act of the highest order, only five or six can be judged in standard I.Q. tests.

Areas that can be judged in I.Q. testing include: general reasoning, memory, vocabulary, and number ability. But other things that relate to creative sciences or creative arts or creative anything are not so easily identified in testing. These include originality, penetration, the ability to redefine, sensitivity to problems, flexibility in thinking, etc.

As most teachers of younger children know, the high I.Q. is not necessarily possessed by the highly creative and talented child, and the creative child is not always blessed with a high I.Q.

Thomas Edison was no academic genius.
Shakespeare was marginally schooled. many of
our best poets, painters, and even scientists were
school drop-outs.

As research reveals the disparity between
measurable intelligence (I.Q.) and performance
intelligence ("non-intelligence intellectual characteristics," as labeled by students of this research), the conclusion seems to be that we need
to redirect our educational systems. We need to
take far more seriously the conclusion that "the
loss of those with high creative ability is greater
than the loss of the highly intelligent and may even
exceed the dropout rate for students in general."

Almost all children are creative.

They are creative, that is, until the growing up process, with its strangling of expression and restric-
tion of freedom, knocks creativity out of them.

**Listening
to Understand
As a Child**

I Corinthians, 13-11, you recall, if taken literally,
could lay the groundwork for downgrading the
child in all of us. "When I was a child I spake as a
child, I understood as a child, I thought as a child.
When I became a man, I put away childish things."
Remember?

What a shame to put away all childish things,
especially the capacity to see, feel, and hear crea-

tively! Creative listening, once stifled in childhood, seldom reappears in the adult. By the time maturity has taken over, the intuitive ability to listen with curiosity is gone. It is replaced most frequently at best by a limited type of listening, fact-oriented or directed to what the person wants to hear only.

Freud, we are reminded by Dr. Roderic Gorney, "described efforts of artists and mystics to recapture the very young child's 'oceanic feeling,' the sense of limitless extension of the self and oneness with the universe."

It is now understood in psychology that the CHILD (or kid) in all of us is the motivation for creative experiences regardless of our chronological age. The ADULT (or mature person) in us provides much of the skill of more technical nature. Dr. Thomas A. Harris says, in *I'm OK – You're OK*, "The Child provides the 'want to' and the Adult provides the 'how to.' " We need the combination of CHILD and ADULT in assertive creative listening, but we can't get far without the CHILD first of all.

Our job as creative listeners is to keep all avenues for receiving outside stimuli open by refusing to "put away childish things" as they relate to the ear and what it hears.

Creative listeners, we could say, are born. But it is up to us to keep the inborn talent for creative listening alive as time goes on, in ourselves, in our children, and in all those we touch in business and other relationships.

Robert Henri said, referring to the creative, child-like part in everyone, "He disturbs, upsets, enlightens, and he opens ways for a better understanding. While those who are not artists are trying to close the book, he opens it, shows there are still more pages possible."

Several leaders in the study of creativity have issued lists of intellectual characteristics of creative people on all age levels. They seem to be shot through with those child-like qualities that we have already suggested. Although we cannot list all of these qualities, in general they converge on a few approaches to receiving and handling stimuli that set the creative person apart from the non-creative. Here are five qualities characteristic of most creative persons, and a word or two about their relation to creative listening.

**Creative Listenin
That Keeps
The Child Alive**

Generally, creative people are:

Alert. They are awake, quick to observe, aware of everything around them. They are unusually sensitive to sights, sounds, smells, how things feel to the touch, tastes. They are open to new experiences, so each new stimulus is freely sent through the nervous system with a minimum of distortion or blockage.

In relation to listening, this means that, instead of receiving sound in predetermined categories ("I hate all poetry, so I won't listen to this," "Classical music is boring," "The sound of her voice drives me nuts"), the assertive listener receives sounds free of rigidity and intolerance.

Playful. The creative person has not lost the capacity to fool around with ideas, stimuli of all kinds. He or she is usually supplied with a good sense of humor; puns, jokes, light verse come easily. Artists play with colors, ideas, and shapes to arrive at something new.

In creative listening, the receiver is toying with sounds to see what ideas they stimulate in association with the frame of reference of the listener. Think of the world of ideas conjured up by Walt Whitman as he listened to all the sounds of his world!

Imaginative. Exploring new ideas, bringing the imagination into full use, is far more appealing to the creative person than carrying out routine tasks.

Creative listeners, also, prefer to imagine new ideas as motivated by what they have heard, rather than take anything "on faith" or purely "as stated."

Constructive. Creative people like to make something new. They are basically builders, not destroyers. But they prefer to build on their own terms, not follow the instructions of others. They prefer to solve problems rather than take readymade solutions. They are problem-centered, not self-centered.

In listening, the creative person will always be applying what he hears to some constructive project, whether it be the creation of a poem or the restructuring of an industry.

Assured. The creative person is assured and assertive in making decisions. This means that creative people are blessed with great ego strength without being egotistically obnoxious. They are prepared to risk failure because they believe in themselves, and they know they can overcome and surmount failure even if faced with it. They are self-confident, autonomous, and independent.

In listening, the creative person will be graced by a talent for asking appropriate questions with assurance, making constructive comments, using listening to keep communication open. The creative listener shows interest in the type of body and face language displayed. He or she receives the message, full of curiosity for what's coming next. So, a sensitive speaker is motivated to rise to meet the challenge of the assured listener, and everyone is saved from a lackluster performance. Creative listeners are seldom bored and they save many situations from becoming boring.

From what we know of creative people — including, of course, creative listeners — they are those who have most completely attained self-actualization. That is, they are stable, optimistic, determined, and generally successful.

Creative Listeners Are Self-Actualized

The psychologist, Abraham Maslow, among his many investigations, studied extensively a group of self-actualized people including Lincoln, Thoreau, Beethoven, Eleanor Roosevelt, and Einstein to see what common characteristics could be discovered in their personalities.

All of them seemed to possess an underlying capacity to listen creatively. They seemed to be assertively creative also in their oral communication, although none of the five examples mentioned has gone down in history as a known word-jammer.

Rather, their ideas, written or verbal, have remained significantly a part of our heritage because they were unique, creative, and, more often than not, expressed in a few, well chosen words.

Creative listeners seldom overburden the world with words anyhow.

They know others can quickly become satiated with the sounds of the human voice, no matter how mellifluous it may be!

Thus Lincoln's Gettysburg Address, one of the shortest ever recorded, continues to be listened to again and again, although its remarkable author predicted most inaccurately, "The world will little note, nor long remember, what we say here. . . ."

Summary   Creative listening has motivated all of the arts, but it can also be a force in all areas of life where communication takes place — business, industry, home, education, etc.

Creative listeners arrive at something new, retaining their child-like ability to listen with their senses. Although there is no very valid testing program, comparable to the I.Q. tests, to evaluate creativity, there are characteristics of creative people which have been observed by a number of researchers in the field. Most of them show a tendency to retain some of the very young child's "oceanic feeling" or kinship with the universe noted by Freud.

In general, creative persons are usually alert, playful, imaginative, constructive, and assured. All of these qualities are reflected in assertive, creative listening.

It may be said that creative listeners are usually self-actualized persons, like Lincoln, Thoreau, Beethoven, Eleanor Roosevelt, and Einstein among others. They use their skills in listening with confidence.

Creative listeners:

Use listening assertively to motivate creative ideas, solutions to problems, etc.

Listen as a child, retaining the child's capacity to receive stimuli without distortion or blockage inflicted by rigidity or stereotyping

Remain, at all times, *Alert, Playful, Imaginative, Constructive,* and *Assured or Assertive.* As a result, they are usually self-actualized people, achieving desired goals by means of creative directions obtained in large part through listening.

Part 3

Winning Results Through Assertive Listening

**Listening to
Lovers, Friends,
and Enemies**

There is no connection between listening assertively to these three — lovers, friends, and enemies!

Did we hear you think that?

You could make a logical case for the common belief that there is absolutely no connection between listening to your girl friend and listening to the old hag down the street who always overcharges at the grocery store and criticizes you when you ask to check the bill.

But you, like debaters often are, would be essentially wrong, no matter how clever, convincing, and logical your arguments might be.

There is a decided similarity in listening to these persons with whom you are associated. In each case, you are communicating on a one-to-one basis, and that makes your end of the communication indispensable. If you aren't listening, nothing is happening.

Second, in the one-to-one relationship with lovers, friends, and enemies, emotions play a weighty role. You are deeply involved and so is the other person. Often, you are part of a two-way love or hate communication. You may love a friend, but not so much nor in quite the same way as a lover. You may also hate a friend, temporarily, but not so intensely as you hate an enemy.

As an assertive listener, your role in all one-to-one relationships is basic to the transaction.

Finally, in most one-to-one relationships you are bartering ideas with the use of what is known as "affective communication." The very words being used are chosen for their "affectiveness." Right now, in this very paragraph, and in much of this book, we use "affective communication, affective words." For example, we involve "you" and we refer to "us" and "we." As S.I. Hayakawa has pointed out in his excellent evaluation of affective communication: "When a speaker or writer feels a special urgency about his message, he can hardly help using . . . the 'personal touch.' "

We can discuss facts, scientific concepts, mathematical formulas most of the time with verbal and non-verbal language that doesn't arouse intense emotional reactions in the other person or persons. But when we talk to lovers, friends, and enemies, we need to know we are dealing in emotions and affective messages. As listeners, we usually are the ones to tune in, and tuning into affective language requires a considerable amount of self-control and self-confidence.

Once, when the Geeting family was in Kashmir, living a week on a houseboat on Lake Dal, attended and cared for by a pleasant host family consisting of the father and two sons, the older, 17-year-old son announced one day that his father had now chosen the girl he was to marry.

Loverly Listening

"Why! Abdul, your father has chosen your bride?" we said, somewhat aghast. "What about your part in the decision?"

"I will be satisfied with my father's decision," said Abdul. "It is the custom in Kashmir."

"Have you met the girl? Do you know what she is like?" we persisted.

"No," the handsome young man replied, "but I will be introduced to her this week. The marriage will take place very soon."

We had imagined such arranged marriages were a thing of the past. But we realized they are not.

Still, our host, the young man's father, recalled a very congenial marriage that had just ended the week before our arrival, when his wife had died. We had wondered where the mother of the boys had gone; but even without her, they had cooked for our family, served us, and tended to our every need.

Our host, who spoke good English, went on to describe a comfortable life with the deceased woman and the satisfaction of having two fine sons. His eyes misted over when he remarked on the closeness of the marriage they had enjoyed for over twenty years.

In the quiet and peace of Lake Dal, they had found a loving relationship, free of the frenzied search for romantic joy. To have survived together, to have had two sons, one now ready for marriage, was more than they had expected out of life. As our host said, with a smile, it had been a very good life and his mate had been a loving wife and mother.

It set us to thinking of the contrast between such a culture and our American, media-dominated society, where falling in love is so closely interwoven with the erotic experience. Here, it is becoming increasingly difficult to recognize true closeness, honest love, and what we have referred to elsewhere in this book as "authentic intimacy."

Dr. Roderic Gorney, in his excellent book, *The Human Agenda,* evaluates pseudo-closeness in the "Fun ethic." He identifies it with *Playboy*-type romance, toplessness, bottomlessness, wife swapping, etc., and says, "All of these kindle a brief flash of erotic fire which, like the flare of a burning pinecone is rapidly exhausted, leaving no lasting warmth. . . ."

The resulting influence of America's new "worship of eroticism" is a society in which thousands of basically miserable human beings are playing a game of gaiety.

Human happiness, self-validation, and satisfaction with life come with an honest, authentic love experience. The "Fun ethic," in Gorney's words, "helps divert energies from physically intimate, enduring love relationships to alienated, transitory, interchangeable pleasure parties . . ." Such experiences tend to diminish the self-validation of the participants and weaken their sense of identity.

But how, you ask, is all this high-sounding talk related to assertive listening?

By now, you have probably begun to understand that trained listening can offer a reliable safeguard against the type of dehumanizing relationship we see masquerading as "love" in society. An assertive listener, who effectively and affectively reacts to physical and mental stimuli with total awareness, will resist a damaging, loveless relationship.

Assertive listening gives you the competence to evaluate body and face language — to determine what in reality lies behind the visual image — and the sensitivity to interpret oral messages accurately.

Assertive listening gives you the talent for unmasking the other person. Most of us wear masks to hide inner feelings. If a person is regaling you with loving sentiments while sitting with tightly crossed arms and legs, you will be cautious about believing what you hear. "I love you," hissed through clenched teeth, doesn't carry the same message as "I love you" uttered in warm, affectionate tones.

Unmasking — the process of removing disciplined facial and body expressions we wear to cover honest inner emotions or to meet expectations of society — must take place before true intimacy between two persons can occur.'

It is not often possible to detect when, and if, a person has bared the real self to reveal the authentic person, unless one is equipped with listening skill. As Julius Fast says in *Body Language,* "Day after day we cover up this bare human being. We hold ourselves in careful control lest our bodies cry out messages our minds are too careless to hide." So, we cover our physical bodies to make ourselves presentable. Women wear brassieres. Men wear tight underwear. Overexposure of sexual organs is thus masked. But when it comes to masking emotions, feelings, and reactions, we can't buy what we need from a commercial supplier.

As we age, the masking of our true selves becomes harder than ever, along with the effort to mask facial sags and wrinkles and body slumping. In the listening process, too, we tend to become less capable. We accept masks with less questioning.

To maintain a lasting love relationship, both partners need to continue to feel self-satisfaction and self-esteem. Love, at best, is a zestful transaction dependent on satisfying communication, especially TLC listening. It can truly flourish only in an atmosphere where this is important, and practiced constantly.

Alexander Pushkin, the Russian poet, said a vital ingredient of any good human exchange is the willingness to listen. Never is this more essential than in the intimate relationship of love.

Listening to Enemies

We can arrive at some interesting slants on listening to enemies by reviewing what certain sages of the past have said.

For example, Ali Ben Abou Taleb, son-in-law of Mahomet and so courageous he was dubbed "The Lion of God," authored a *Hundred Sayings* before he was murdered in A.D. 660. Among them (in translation by James Russell Lowell) we find this:

> "He who has a thousand friends has not a friend to spare, And he who has one enemy will meet him everywhere."

Thomas Middleton, who died in the early 17th century, wrote a play with the appealing title, *Anything for a Quiet Life,* in which he refers to "my nearest and dearest enemy."

But it took Dante Gabriel Rossetti, painter and poet who died less than a hundred years ago, to question:

> "Was it a friend or foe that spread these lies? It was one of my most intimate enemies."

The concept of "intimate," "dearest," ever-present enemies in these examples makes it clear that people have always dealt very personally with enemies. Part of being human, no doubt, is having real or imagined enemies. Even Benjamin Franklin, ennobled in history as a reasonable, mature man, said in a letter to William Strahan, July 5, 1775, "You and I were long friends: you are now my enemy, and I am yours."

A number of years ago, I (Baxter) was involved in the establishment and building of one of the largest state universities in California. I came in "on the ground floor" at Sacramento, and my position as Chairman of the Humanities and Fine Arts Division called for considerable vision, risk, responsibility, and money.

A number of projects I felt demanded immediate initiation, to put the university on the map, involved heavy expenditures for suitable buildings, equipment, and even what might have appeared frivolous ideas like superior mural decorations on outside walls.

The university was fortunate in having a competent and cautious officer in charge of finance. But we became almost bitter enemies. It seemed to me everything I thought we must have was scratched from the budget.

Finally, one day I had a brilliant thought. I would go to this guy's office and start some kind of personal communication.

"Van," I said, "you and I are both deeply involved in the building of an institution. But we seem to be turning into enemies over dollar issues. How about our meeting regularly to think things through, together? You talk to me. I'll listen. Then I'll talk to you. You listen."

"Good idea," said Van, and we started meeting once a week for lunch.

Much to my surprise, Van turned from the uptight, narrowminded person I had imagined into a reasonable, flexible, and thoroughly responsible officer. As we continued listening, talking, and munching our sandwiches, we developed an understanding and appreciation of each other. Our friendship over the years has continued warm and mutually respectful.

Through the rather simple technique of listening without prejudice, listening to the end, withholding judgment until all ideas and facts were in, we mellowed and gave in, each of us, enough to arrive at basic decisions for the university that would not have been possible had we remained enemies. The well-equipped buildings we needed came into being, along with the murals to give them class. And the budget weathered it all in good shape. Van and I still smile when we think of our narrow escape from permanent estrangement.

On the other hand, I have a fine enemy. He's one of the best artists in the community, whose paintings I much admire but don't wish to own because of a bitter experience that arose over very faulty listening. To this day, we haven't resolved a problem that arose almost twenty years ago. He has a thousand friends and so have I, but we each have one "intimate," "dearest" enemy — each other. It serves to remind me, I have work to do in assertive listening!

The term, "emotional filters," has been used by listening teachers for many years. We think it originated with that eminent Professor of Rhetoric, Dr. Ralph G. Nichols, who pioneered much research on all aspects of listening.

Handling Emotional Filters in Listening

It is a term particularly applicable to the consideration of listening to others on a one-to-one basis, like lovers and enemies. How hard it is to listen to a "liberal" Democrat if you're a "right-wing" Republican and vice versa! How hard to listen to a Jew if you're an Arab! How difficult to listen to a Woman's Libber if you're "just a housewife" by choice!

We suffer from what Nichols calls "emotional deafness" when we meet the lover or the enemy face to face, but for different reasons. We want very much to believe the lover. We want very much to distrust the enemy.

Nichols recalls a story of a women convicted of murder, sentenced to die in the electric chair. Her big worry as she approached death was missing a segment of the soap opera scheduled after her death! The serial's producers heard the story and sent her a synopsis of the upcoming season, so she could have her dying wish fulfilled — to know how it all came out! Such is the control of emotional involvement. But we all have strong emotional ties and controls, no matter how much we believe ourselves to be on a mature (ADULT) level.

Nichols reminds us of the tricky problems encountered when we fail to appreciate the impact of emotional filters in listening.

He offers three good ways of avoiding emotionally warped listening.

First, "withhold evaluation," of course.

Second, "hunt for negative evidence" in your own thinking as well as that of the other person. "If you make up your mind to seek out the ideas that might prove you wrong, as well as those that might prove you right, you are less in danger of missing what people have to say."

Third, "make a realistic self-analysis." This means, search yourself for the cause of problems if you find the other person steps on your mental toes, causing you emotional distress.

Summary

Listening to lovers, friends, and enemies has three elements in common: (1) it is one-to-one on a more or less intimate level, (2) it is charged with emotion a large part of the time, and (3) it is characterized by the use of "affective communication" aimed at a more personal approach.

Assertively listening to lovers can help in establishing "authentic intimacy" and in avoiding pseudo-closeness so evident in the "Fun ethic" society, dominated by the "worship of eroticism." Assertive listening helps in avoiding damaging, loveless relationships and in arriving at the zestful transaction, true love, so dependent on satisfying, self-validating communication.

Assertively listening to enemies, encouraging an honest exchange of ideas, often can succeed in overcoming ill-founded prejudice and in relieving misunderstandings.

Dealing with friends, enemies, and lovers in one-to-one communication demands skill in "unmasking" visual fronts and listening through "emotional filters" that warp messages.

The assertive listener, communicating with lovers, friends, and enemies:
Pays close attention to the *affective* elements in verbal and non-verbal exchange
Avoids pseudo-closeness and seeks authentic intimacy in loved ones.

Applications

Family Listening

Much of this discussion concerns Judy, for listening in her family could have saved a very tragic situation.

Judy is a 17-year-old high school senior suffering from an unhappy relationship with her parents. When things get too bad at home, she (like 6,000 other frustrated teenagers in Sacramento County, California, alone) runs away from home. Twenty-five percent of these runaways are repeaters!

As reported in the *Sacramento Bee,* fall, 1975, Judy's problem was mainly no listening at home. "Finally I get frustrated," she says, "and I get a sick feeling in my gut. I rip a book apart to get rid of my aggressions. . . . I feel like hitting my head against the wall. I can't take it any more." So she runs away. This conversation with her took place on her third truancy from home within the year.

Analyzing the problem, "Authorities say Judy's case is typical — there is little, if any, communication at home," according to the reporter.

A deputy probation officer working in the county's Family Crisis Intervention Unit said, "The kids try to talk to their parents, but *the parents don't hear what the kids are saying.*" (Emphasis ours.)

Judy describes her home situation: "I get along fine with my mother during the day. . . . Then she drinks a lot after 5 o'clock . . . you might say she's an alcoholic. When my father comes home they usually ignore each other. But they take out their aggressions on me. They yell at me . . . They don't let me have a say in anything."

Judy is part of a national problem of runaways estimated to be "nearly a million kids every year." And runaways are getting younger. Many are 11- and 12-year-olds. Nationwide, the average age of runaways is around fourteen, according to FBI statistics.

A representative of Sacramento's Youth Services Division, pursuing the analysis of Judy's problem, says, "The important thing is to get the parents and the kid talking. The main thing is to get some communication going . . . on both sides." He is referring to Parents and Children, in speaking of both sides.

Judy's problem leads to the question of the family as an institution in America. How endangered is the family?

How Endangered Is The Family?

According to New York psychoanalyst, Herbert Hendin, "Nothing says more about the American family than how painful a subject it has become . . . much of family life over the past 20 years has become a paradigm of discontent."

Hendin points to results of his study of hundreds of students, college age, over the past six years. The students were chosen at random.

Among the more alarming revealed facts are these: The suicide rate among the youth has risen more than 250 percent in the past twenty years. Drug abuse has peaked and leveled off at a shockingly high level. Despite the sexual openness beyond anything known in our 200-year history, anger between the sexes and impotence in college man have reached unprecedented heights. Finally, Hendin notes with alarm, "Nothing distinguishes this generation of young men more than the degree to which they are irresistibly drawn to *killing feeling* as a means of survival." (Emphasis ours).

Listening— The Untried Solution to Family Ills

If the American family is to be spared the fate of the dodo bird, it is high time to pay careful attention to the threatened extinction of communication, *especially listening,* within the family structure. Hendin's findings help illuminate the problem breaking up Judy's family. At the basis of all these family ills is lack of human concern.

Without doubt, a renaissance of listening, in all its aspects, could restore the family and place it on a more stable basis than it has ever known in the nation's history. And this could be accomplished without taking away equality of rights or endangering any of the valuable ground gained in the woman's movement these past ten years.

But listening as a solution to family ills has not been spotlighted. Yet.

Like penicillin, the discovery of which re-volutionized efforts to control infection, or vaccina-tion, which has almost entirely stamped out smallpox in the world, LISTENING could be the great remedy within the family.

Assertive listening, if practiced in all its aspects and with studied skill — listening to learn what problems are, listening creatively in solving them, listening analytically to discover specific family needs, listening always with Tender Loving Care to help each famly member — could be the source of reconstructing the family and placing it on a higher plane than humankind has experi-enced in its long, jagged history of the family as an institution.

Listening to Children

It's never too early to start the human being listen-ing. Listening is an acquired skill, although re-search by Dr. Lee Salk shows that recordings of adult heartbeats and blood rushing through the uterus lull newborn infants, and recordings of the soft whooshing sound of the womb have proven effective in soothing premature babies.

Children are taught to chew with mouths closed, to say good morning, goodbye, please, and thank you, but most parents allow them to grow up never experiencing the opportunity to learn basic skills and the general courtesy of listening. Surely, lis-tening is seldom taught in the family as a positive life force!

Parents who are often good listeners in adult company, pay slight attention to their children when they have something to say. Yet parents are disappointed, or even disbelieving, when their children grow up without consideration for "their elders."

Dr. Ralph G. Nichols, who initiated research among college students with regard to early home life, found the better listeners came from families where parents had respected and encouraged listening. They had, in fact, revered it. Nichols contends that the ear "needs experience" and says, "When a child's listening activities are allowed to develop without occasional guidance, they are almost certain to gravitate toward easier and easier listening." Later, in school, such children find "a great deal of learning must come through listening to lectures which require considerable mental exertion." If the capacity to listen to learn, to listen analytically, has been built into the family background, the child will have an advantage.

As for family ties, Nichols observes, "When emphasis is placed on hearing and understanding one another at home, words that are spoken give strength to family ties that can last forever."

But what really is happening with listening in some families today?

How often in the grocery store have we heard children whine, "Can I have this candy bar?" "I want some bubble gum." "What'ch gonna get me for being good?" And instead of considering the child's basic need for attention, the harried Dad or Mom ignores the requests completely. Then, we hear the whine develop into a clamor for attention. Then mount to a rude demand. The parent awakens with a start and shouts, "For heaven's sake, will you stop shouting! No, I won't get you a damned thing!"

Not only has the child learned that his efforts, at first reasonably mild perhaps, get no attention, he has been exposed to an adult acting like a spoiled brat!

Basic appreciation of the great human need to be listened to, which begins almost at birth and which is exceedingly strong in children, might have prevented this unhappy exchange, so damaging both to parent and child. Listening in the family, assertive listening, could have changed their lives.

Children, we know from reliable research, are strongly influenced by what happens to them before they are five. By this age, patterns are established, including listening patterns. If they are to learn to listen and to respect listening, they must be introduced to it in the home, in the family.

Nothing replaces the presence of effective role models. Parents or baby-sitters, grandmas and grandpas, can have an impact on listening habits built into children. If the young see listening respected in the family circle, among members of the supervisorial staff — like Mom and Dad — they are more apt to want to listen themselves. Children are great mimics.

To be good listeners, humans of all ages, especially children, need to be listened to. Really listened to. Not just stared at vacantly.

"Dad! Guess what I just saw on television. . . ." says Jill, running into Dad's study. Maybe he is busy at the moment. Maybe he is on the telephone, handling an important business problem at home. What may he do to help Jill become a good listener?

He might say to the person on the phone, "Pardon me a moment," and then turn to Jill and say, "Hey, Hon, I can't wait to hear about what you saw, but I must finish discussing something with this person on the phone. I'll be through very soon, and then we can hear all about it. . . ."

As soon as possible, he should make good the promise. He should take time to listen with real curiosity, not faked, to Jill. At this important moment, Dad is building in a vital listening lesson by demonstrating effective listening himself. Jill will reward him by being a child who has respect for the most important part of communication — listening.

Dominick A. Barbara, psychoanalyst, says: "The art of listening begins at home. . . . For parents, listening in the early years of a child's growth depends not just on the fact of being quiet and attentive. Of even greater importance is the conveyance of a sympathetic and whole-hearted attitude of acceptance."

There are some situations ideal for listening activity in family life.

Situations for Family Listening

Listening within the family circle at dinner time, giving each child a fair share of concerned attention, showing respect for his or her contributions, is a daily experience from which lifelong listeners are born. Also, at dinner, children should be encouraged to listen attentively to Mom and Dad, Grandma and Grandpa, and guests. This is as important as being heard.

Another family activity is reading aloud. Many strong family groups still read daily from the Bible, read stories to the young (and, in turn, let the young read to the grown-ups), and read aloud bits from the daily newspapers of interest to the family.

Quarrels afford excellent listening opportunities. Although quarrels between parents and children can be prevented (but should not be), it is the way they are handled that marks the child in adulthood. A child who has his or her own point of view listened to in a family quarrel, and who, in turn, has been encouraged to listen to the parent's (or other family member's) side, is on the way to being a better parent sometime in the future. And the well-listened-to child, in a family quarrel, will often be saved from becoming the rebellious teenager, like Judy, who gives up and runs away from home.

Outlawing discipline, however, is not a means of encouraging the maturing of good listeners. Sometimes children do not understand or react to a mild suggestion. Parental authority, at these times, gives to the child a feeling of stability.

Balancing the swing to permissiveness in the 1930-1950 era, which encouraged a minimum of demands and restrictions on the child, we now seem to have a swing in the direction of renewed respect for a measure of strictness in parents.

Dr. Stanley Coopersmith, psychologist at the Davis campus of the University of California, participated in a recent study of parental authority and reported: "The strict parents granted their child more responsibility, *listened to him more closely,* even when he spoke of unimportant matters, knew virtually all of his friends, gave him a say in making family plans, and were able to tolerate sharp disagreements with him." (Emphasis ours.) Interpretation of the word "strict," of course, is in the ear of the listener, but it would indicate that, as used, it means being deeply concerned about, and interested in, the child. Listening to the child is the parents' means of understanding that child and knowing how far they can go in limiting and encouraging his or her individuality.

There is considerable difference between listening to the child analytically to discover hidden problems that may be triggering his disposition upsets, and listening to him with Tender Loving Care to help him discover his own needs, wishes, and desires. There is also a difference between listening creatively to an excited, imaginative child, helping her to bring out of her observations some wonderful bit of verse or picture or song, and listening to her to learn what she discovered at school today to extend her knowledge in math or reading or social studies.

Wise and wonderfully assertive listening parents will not often be disappointed in the adult that matures from their little offspring.

Listening to Husbands and Wives

Remember how Judy described her parents' relationship? When her father got home her mother was already braced with alcohol. They ignored each other. They took out their hostility on Judy. What each person in this marriage relationship lacked was the capacity to listen to the other.

Dr. Carl Rogers (in *On Becoming a Person*) speaks of family relationships and how they depend on the freedom to express true feelings, knowing that each person (as in the case of Judy's mother and father) will receive messages with calm understanding.

Rogers makes a well substantiated point through many illustrations from his experience as a psychotherapist: "When we are living behind a facade, when we are trying to act in ways that are not in accord with our feelings, then *we dare not listen freely to another."* (Emphasis ours) He explains that as a result of coming to terms with yourself (understanding your selves, as further explained in Chapter 16 you are "no longer on the defensive and . . . can really listen to, and understand, another member of [your] family." This is because you "can see how life appears to this other person."

Permitting your husband or your wife to have honest feelings, to be "a separate person," as Dr. Rogers says, is what he calls "a most radical step." He speaks of the tremendous pressures we often put on a husband or a wife to have the same feelings we have. It is as if we said, "If you want my love, you have to believe what I believe, like what I like, and do what I do." That is the beginning of marriage breakdown. (It is also the beginning of generation gap when parents expect children to repeat their lifestyles.)

Listening assertively to one's mate is the road to understanding and the basis of authentic love. It must begin with casting off one's own defenses. To do that, says Dr. Rogers, you must first have respect for yourself and assertively believe you are "a responsible and self-directing individual."

Listening, in all its ramifications, is the key to understanding the feelings of your husband or wife. With understanding comes mutual regard. And honest relationships.

Applications

Some families are blessed, or cursed, with grand-parents. It depends largely on how well the senior citizen listens.

Listening to the Senior Citizen

This specialized group of older people is increasing rapidly in our society, due to improved diet and better medication and the will to live.

While the male comes in for much ribbing and the female is often referred to as "the little old lady in tennis shoes," something is happening to them, both male and female. They are finding their voices, speaking up on their own behalf, forming formidable groups, like the Gray Panthers.

Great! But what about the improvement of their listening styles?

Probably no group in the family circle so abuses the privilege of verbalizing as do the older persons. Because of long and at times distinguished careers, they feel amply qualified to conduct endless monologues beginning, "When I was. . . ."

If you are over 55 or 60 and hear yourself doing this already, you may understand why the young are turning away from you.

On the other hand, you may still believe (as they do in oriental societies) that the older people get, the wiser. It's time to wise up to the power of assertive listening to win back your family.

With older age comes a certain deterioration in hearing. Often, to make up for this, the older persons talk more. They say to themselves, "If I can still talk so well, I must be very much alive, destined to live quite a few more active years." A switch to more listening and less talking would bring far more happy attention.

It is never too late to start listening — assertively. That is, with active concern. Listening, in all its dimensions described in this book, can change the lives of senior citizens for the better. It can put them "back in touch" with younger family members. Assertive listeners, no matter how old, are very much in demand in our society. Welcome in any age group. Everyone loves a listener!

As one old fellow put it, when he started positive assertive listening at age 80, "I never knew what fun listening could be! Now the young ones seem to like me. Don't make much difference if I am getting a wee deaf. I don't really need to hear perfectly to be a perfectly good listener!"

Listening is the passport to a better life in the senior citizen category. A truly active listening grandparent can bridge the generation gap, no matter how many years lie between him or her and younger members of the family.

Think of what a well-equipped-for-listening grandfather could mean in the family! Carl Rogers, in speaking of the concept of trusting the individual to be himself, said, "I sometimes fantasy about what it would mean if a child were treated in this fashion from the first. Suppose a child were permitted to have his own unique feelings — suppose he never had to disown his feelings in order to be loved. . . . It would mean the child would grow up respecting himself as a unique person. . . . He would be relatively free of the maladjustments which cripple so many of us."

What a marvelous legacy a listening grandpa could leave his grandchild. "I remember my grandfather as a truly wonderful listener," his grandson would one day recall. "He listened to me and especially to my feelings when I was little. He helped me to become a responsible and self-directed person. I can't place a value on his gift of listening. It was priceless, and he gave it so freely."

Could any grandfather ask for more by way of memorial?

As we allow each individual in the family to be a separate person — each child, each parent, each grandparent — the family circle closes around a fully functioning group of individuals. Listening within the circle can bring about this miracle of affection and warmth.

The Family Circle, Marked by Separateness

Real feelings, not masked or faked, are brought to the surface and encouraged to develop. Each person in the circle becomes a bona fide Human Being. Respected and loved. Allowed to be different. And, above all, listened to by every other member of the group.

In the listening process, as Rogers reminds us, each family member is helped to discover the true self, and to become himself or herself with family blessing and approval.

Even Judy. Who would never run away from such a family!

Summary

It has been said that "much of family life over the past 20 years has become a paradigm of discontent" and we have numerous illustrations of the results of such discontent, including runaway teenagers, rising suicide rates among the youth, drug abuse, and a general feeling of "copping out" noted in certain segments of our society.

Listening assertively within the family could solve many of the ills feeding into the patterns of deterioration.

Listening begins in early childhood and is strongly established in family relationships at all ages, young to very old. Situations for family listening include: Dinner-hour communication, reading aloud in the family circle, and handling of quarrels and disagreements. But discipline is not ruled out in parent-child relationships as listening is encouraged. Rather, strict parents have been found to "listen more closely" than those exhibiting scant parental authority.

In family listening between husband and wife, parent and child, younger family members and grandparents, etc., each individual is encouraged to be a "separate" and fully functioning individual, respected and loved for his or her unique qualities.

Assertive listening in the family means:

Establishing authentic relationships between husband and wife, parent and child, and younger family members and grandparents

Assisting each individual to be fully functioning, separate, and his or her own true self, within the family circle

Preventing many social problems such as drug abuse, runaway among teenagers, rising suicide rates, and "cop out" lifestyles.

Applications

**Listening in
Business
and Industry**

Betty McKuen manages a large complex of apartments. She says the job is one part business management and nine parts human management.

Listening is a big part of Betty's job.

She says it starts the moment a prospective renter appears. At that point she begins forming opinions and making judgments about placing the person in her complex. She tries to listen to discover the type of person or persons who might be renters. Are they young? College age? Have they children or are they childless? Are they older? Will they be sensitive to noise? Will neighbors with hi-fi's bother them? What part of the apartment complex might be most suitable to their needs?

Even after renting to people, Betty must stay on the listening alert to keep things moving smoothly — listening to complaints, requests, excuses, and even threats. At times she listens as a confidante. One elderly lady calls every day to have something fixed or inspected.

"But really she is lonely, this old lady," says Betty. "There is little wrong. She just wants to come in and chat a bit. Part of my job as a successful landlady is to listen with Tender Loving Care when it's needed. It is part of being a good manager."

While Betty McKuen's business is managing an apartment complex, what she knows about listening can be of great value to managers in any kind of business or industry.

Listening Begins at The Top

A mysterious illness recently struck fifty employees of a big hospital in California. Although at first it seemed to be caused by a "virus-like agent," extensive laboratory tests ruled this out. Then, the state epidemiologist, Dr. Brian Boni, offered a most interesting possible explanation. He said that in his opinion "overwork and stress related to labor negotiations" could cause such an epidemic, that it could stem from "psychosomatic illness" caused by "low morale and overwork, as well as personality conflicts and personnel disagree-

Applications

ments." To support his theory he cited research showing mass hysteria as the cause of similar outbreaks in 1957 and 1959 among groups of nurses in Montana.

We wonder how far careful listening in labor disputes (such as those which preceded the mysterious illness in California) could go in solving, preventing, or alleviating the breakdowns in large employee groups rather frequently reported in our society.

Successful managers of whatever group know how to listen skillfully, whether consciously or unconsciously. Highly successful managers have mastered the uses of assertive listening styles and know when and how to listen for facts, to listen analytically, to listen creatively, and last, but certainly not least in importance, when and how to listen with Tender Loving Care. Each type of listening has its place, often overlapping within a short span of time. But the best manager is equipped with all listening skills and can use them when needed.

A famous study made some time ago by researchers at Loyola University sought the answer to just one question: What is the single most important attribute of an effective manager? Thousands of workers were questioned about this, and the results were summarized as follows:

"Of all the sources of information a manager has, by which he can come to know and accurately size up the personalities of the people in his department, listening to the individual employees is the most important. The most stereotyped report we have received from thousands of workers who testified they like their supervisor was this one: 'I like my boss, he listens to me, I can talk to him.' "

Perhaps a story will explain the importance of managers really listening. Here is a report of an actual encounter between foreman Bill and his supervisor.

The supervisor, who had called Bill to his office, explained what he hoped might be a change in Bill's department. A casting, the supervisor felt, would work better than a hand-forged job. He explained how it should be made. But Bill was quiet.

"Oh yeah?" Bill finally said, hesitantly.

Now, it was possible to interpret that comment in various ways. Bill seemed to be freezing up, as the supervisor continued. "I wonder what is the matter with Bill?" he asked himself as he saw Bill's stern look. "Is he just dumb or am I not making myself clear?"

Then the supervisor sensed Bill might have something to say. So he said: "Bill, you've been in the department longer than I have. What is your reaction to my suggestion? I'm listening."

Bill paused and then he began to talk since the boss had opened the door to communication. He offered some highly experienced and sound advice. The supervisor found it helpful and decided Bill was smarter than he had thought. Bill came to the conclusion that his boss was pretty smart himself. A mutual respect and trust developed. Listening had paved the way for improved communication and a good solution to the technical problem of the casting. The supervisor, we might point out, while listening, remained in complete control of the situation. He was an assertive, not passive, listener.

Enlightened listening should begin at the top. The president of a company can provide a role model for the personnel of the entire organization by respecting listening and encouraging its enlightened use in all communication at all levels. Nothing encourages cooperation within a business or industry so dramatically as good listening, all the way — top to bottom, bottom to top!

Assertive Listening Is Good Business All The Way

Charles C. Vance, a Chicago management consultant, writing in *Nation's Business* tells how a boss "can ruin or lose a junior executive with the wrong kind of reprimand." But he also tells how "matters can be handled so that both the firm and the young manager win."

Briefly, Vance lists five basic patterns of straightening out a young manager: "Storm at the man, humiliate him, teach him a lesson," "Stare the man down, threaten to fire him," "Show the man he's low on the totem pole by comparing him with the peer competition he fears," "Warn him to make changes, but in such a quiet voice the warning isn't heard." There are four suggestions. But listen to the fifth: "Tell him you want to hear his side of the story, and listen."

"And listen," says Vance. The junior executive then hears something like this: "We need comers of your type; we need your enthusiasm and capabilities. You just ran into a small procedural problem. Here is what you can do to straighten things out and avoid such occasions in the future."

As Vance points out, the young manager is given needed help, but he leaves "feeling he has had a reasonable day in court."

Even better, though, is having a manager do his research — to know, before meeting the younger man, what his "innermost" thoughts, fears, and attitude might be. Not only should the manager listen, he should prepare himself (having done his homework) to make valuable suggestions concerning goals, further schooling, and accountability to one's self. The senior officer who backs his listening time with this preparation for personal encounter will save young persons from failure and put them on the road to becoming "top management material for the years ahead." Listening is at the heart of it, though.

One of the classic studies made by the Savage-Lewis Corporation of Minneapolis, an advertising and communications firm often referred to by Dr. Ralph G. Nichols, concerns the fall-off in communication efficiency as you go down the levels of management in American business and industry. This study of 100 representative business and industrial managements showed fairly good rapport between members of the board at the top (there are usually five levels of management). One director talking with another may achieve 90 percent efficiency. Foremen talking to other foremen get along well too. But, as you start down the line and a board chairman calls on a vice-president, for example, only 67 percent of the communication is going to be received accurately. The vice-president talking to the general supervisor is going to get only 56 percent of his message understood; the supervisor talking to the plant manager will achieve only 40 percent communication. To the foreman, only 30 percent gets across and, down the line to the worker, the message suffers a breakdown that allows it to be received at only 20 percent understanding. Dr. Nichols asks, "How can an outfit operate on 20 percent efficiency in communication?" And answers the question, "The horrible truth is, it cannot! That's why most of us are headed for bankruptcy." And, capping his point, Nichols quotes statistics to show that "every 25 years, some 90 percent of all American businesses go bankrupt."

What happens to the worker who receives so little communication from the top? Who must, therefore, feel almost completely "out of touch" with the company he works for?

Characteristically, he is tempted to feel cheated, unconcerned, lacking in loyalty. Resulting behavior by way of retaliation may be to steal, stay home sick, or slow up on the job.

Morale is based on self-esteem. If the worker is not given adequate concern by his superiors, he will seek some form of revenge.

Once when I (Baxter) was connected with a major food chain in the United States, authoring guides and manuals in the home office, there was a problem with employee morale in the Los Angeles area. It took the form of a demand for major increases in salary, not possible at the time. Management imagined the real cause of distress might be due to bad rest-room facilities, especially in the women's area. It was almost ready to launch a massive redecoration and enlargement program, adding showers, etc., when someone said, "Say, I wonder if that is really the underlying cause of discontent."

There was a feeling such a costly program should not be undertaken without some research, so a team of student-researchers from U.C.L.A. was brought into the picture. These young people interviewed, with questionnaires, some 800 employees who had most recently quit the company. (The turnover at this point was terrific.) And they made a most surprising discovery.

The true source of unhappiness, they found, was not in rest-rooms or salary level. Employee morale had slipped to a real low due to lack of communication, especially in not listening to individual employees to find what their problems were. As these employees were interviewed, the consensus was neatly summarized in a statement like, "Nobody up there seems to hear a thing I've been saying. What really bugs me is the miscellaneous transfer going on, from store to store, as if I could just move every other week. It is nothing to be called and told, 'You're being transferred to . . . tomorrow.' It might mean I have to take a bus clear across town, or move. I tried to get through to my supervisor, but nobody was listening."

Once the problem was diagnosed, the correction was fairly simple. A firm policy went into force immediately against "miscellaneous transfer" and a program to train supervisors in communication techniques was launched. Within one year the personnel turnover, which had been at the rate of 135 percent per year had been lowered to 60 percent per year. The company saved thousands of dollars in training of new personnel costs alone; the rest-rooms were cleaned up but not re-volutionized; and salaries were improved but not to the point of bankrupting the company. Overall costs were more than compensated for by getting involved in what Dr. Nichols has referred to as "upward communication," getting messages from employee to top management.

As was found in one research study of twenty-four industrial plants, "morale factors" that employees considered most important and ranked 1, 2, and 3 (1, full appreciation of work done; 2, feeling "in" on things; and 3, sympathetic help on personal problems) were just reversed in ranking order by top (non-listening) management and placed 8, 9, and 10 respectively.

Of greatest importance to the employee was GRATITUDE — full appreciation for what he had done!

Interesting, too, that Dr. Hans Selye, leading Canadian doctor and distinguished authority on living with STRESS, gives as a key to relieving stress, the expression of gratitude. Expressing gratitude, he says, contributes to peace of mind, security, and personal fulfillment. All the more reason for management to heed the worker's need for thanks, when it has been earned.

Aids to Management Through Listening

There are helpful materials available to managers concerning the general principles of good and bad listening. Many of these boil down to lists of one kind or the other, including:

"Commandments of Good Communication" (which includes listening as #10)

"Commandments for Good Listening"

"Mental Manipulations"

"Do's of Listening"

"Objectives of Listening"

"Listening Techniques"

These lists range in number from 3 to 10, usually.

Also, there are lists approaching the problem from the negative side. These include: "Ten Bad Habits of Listening" and Ralph Nichols' famous "Ten Worst Listening Habits," introduced by him several years ago. Briefly, they include:

1. Calling the subject uninteresting.
2. Criticizing delivery.
3. Getting overstimulated.
4. Listening only for facts.
5. Trying to outline everything you hear.
6. Faking attention.
7. Tolerating audience distractions.
8. Evading difficult material.
9. Letting emotion-laden words get between you and the speaker.
10. Wasting the differential between speech speed and thought speed.

(Regarding the last point he says the average

American talks at the rate of 135 words per minute and may slow down to 100 words per minute in making a speech. But people listen at "an easy cruising speed of at least 400 words per minute" and tune in and out to most speeches as a consequence of the differential between the speed of sound and speed of thought.)

Some of the important areas in which management must begin to listen with the new process and skills made clear in this book include such overlooked everyday activities as Meetings, Telephone Communication, and Personal Encounters.

Take Meetings first. How many managers have studied the role of listening (particularly listening for information and analytical listening) in meeting management? Listening in problem solving and decision making in meetings cannot be overemphasized, but it is seldom mentioned in any instructional manuals relating to democratic procedures for group decisions.

In making group decisions, the individual's commitment is to the group's decision. There must be an opportunity for all to express opinions and ideas (for "brainstorming"); but, uncontrolled, such episodes can get out of hand. Management must know how to listen for danger signals, at the same time providing ample opportunity for free expression of opinion.

In meetings, it is necessary to make very clear all ideas or facts that might be fed into a decision.

Managers must listen carefully to be sure each group member knows what is being discussed and acted upon. To effect this clarity, questions are often a magic key. Good questions elicit information, save time, and move meetings ahead. Managers need to know how to shape questions to get facts, ideas, and opinions without encouraging endless monologues on the part of members who would talk interminably.

Finally, an atmosphere for problem solving should be free of anger and emotion, fear and intimidation. A skilled manager knows all about listening for signals that would indicate members of the group are uncomfortable, and seeks to improve the atmosphere before it deteriorates. Skilled managers take all possible steps to see that everyone in the group has a fair share of talking time. Carefully constructed agendas guard against a good many impossible communication situations that arise because people aren't listening and overtalk.

Telephone communication is overlooked as an important part of management listening because it is assumed that everyone knows how to listen on the telephone. There is a void in the available training programs on this important subject.

Nowhere else does the "tone of voice" make such an immediate impression as it does on the telephone. It substitutes for all the non-verbal signals not available — the body and face language signals, gestures, smiles, frowns, etc., discussed earlier in this book. A good manager will approach each phone call with an image in mind of the person he wants to project. And, if he is a listening manager, it will be an image of an efficient but relaxed person, honest, concerned, interested, constructive, helpful. Being in control of the techniques of assertive listening, he will project confidence that he can be helpful, can make good decisions, and can, before making them, listen to all the facts.

And speaking of "tone of voice," managers need to listen to themselves on record or tape to analyze what is being heard when they open their mouths. If the voice is too low, they may be making others uncomfortable by forcing them to ask for a repetition of a message. On the other hand, if a voice is too loud, it may be intimidating or too exciting to others.

One student in a listening seminar told of his biggest problem as a new deputy on the sheriff's department, that of getting cooperation from jail inmates in listening to him. He spent several months shouting louder and louder, getting more and more sore throats. One day, he decided to try some advice given him by a senior deputy. He spoke almost in a whisper. Immediately, the inmates silenced. From that time on, he said, he remembered to whisper his instructions, and "the results were fantastic. The inmates listened and I had fewer sore throats."

Personal encounters are a part of every manager's day. Good and helpful managers spend time getting to know the people in their organization. But personal encounters based on the manager's saying "Hi, Charley, how are you?" and not stopping long enough to find out, are worse than none.

Listening in all its aspects (again we think of listening for information, to provide Tender Loving Care, etc.) is the magic key to getting along well with, and helping, others.

A "jolly boy," "hale fellow well met," "slap on the back" manager doesn't fit the modern idiom of "good boss."

No, the manager who is liked, respected, and listened to is the one who begins by listening. And listening in the appropriate way — never aggressively, always assertively.

In personal encounters which go beyond the casual hello and how's the family? stage, there are some listening techniques which may be used to great advantage. They have been suggested by

Dr. Robert K. Burns of the University of Chicago
and seem particularly useful. Some examples are
summarized:

When managers want clarification or additional
facts, they can ask such questions as: "Can you
clarify this?" or "Is this the problem as you see it
now?"

*When managers want to check their understand-
ing* and listening accuracy or encourage further
discussion, they can ask questions like: "As I understand it, then, your plan is . . . (restatement) . . .
am I hearing you correctly?"

When managers want to stay neutral but show
their interest and give encouragement, they can
say things like: "I see," "Uh-huh," or "I get the
idea."

When managers want to be reflective and show
they understand the other's feelings, they can
make comments like: "You felt you didn't get a fair
shake?"

When managers want to summarize, to focus on
main points of discussion or offer a springboard
for further consideration of problems, they can
comment with such remarks as: "If I understand
what you have been saying about the situation
. . ." (and summarize).

The field for improving management, all up and
down the line, through listening, has barely been
scratched. But in some ways that is good; it leaves
the challenge open to imaginative and creative
management to come up with some new techniques.

Enlightened companies are discovering that listening can be a powerful antidote to communication illnesses. It is a creative force and a stabilizing control agent, if it is practiced assertively by all employees, beginning at the top.

Summary

Successful managers know how to listen skillfully with all the types of assertive listening described in this book. Research has revealed that employees consider listening a top priority in management.

Although enlightened listening must begin at the top, there is a vast need for improvement in listening all down the line — from management through to worker and from worker back through to management. Assertive listening is good business all the way.

Unhappy employees (not listened to) tend to feel cheated, unconcerned, and lacking in loyalty, and to retaliate in some way.

Important areas for management and employees to listen include Meetings, Telephone Communication, and Personal Encounters, all of which require a variety of listening skills. Enlightened companies are discovering that listening can be a powerful antidote to communication illnesses, a creative force, and a stabilizing control agent, if practiced assertively by all — top to bottom, and vice versa.

Assertive listening in business and industry
means:

Developing all types of listening skill, beginning
with top management and carrying through to employee level

Using listening as a communication tool in all
areas of company confrontation, particularly in
meetings and personal encounters. Telephone listening is of major importance, also.

**Listening
in Politics and
Government**

Soon after her inauguration as Connecticut's first woman governor, Ella T. Grasso did a memorable thing.

AP wirephoto flashed a picture of her doing it, which appeared in papers coast to coast.

It was captioned: THE GOVERNOR LISTENS.

It shows a well groomed older woman, who has removed her shoes and tucked them away beside her comfortable office sofa, listening to a couple of concerned men. They are leaning forward, gesturing hands extended. Talking.

But Governor Grasso is sitting back listening, attentively.

No one has accused her of being weak, lacking in assertiveness. She is quite capable of making forthright and bold statements, of speaking up when the situation demands it. But the thing that distinguishes her from many of her male counterparts is her courage to listen.

Does Anyone Listen in Public Office?

Leo Rosten, in a TV interview with Eric Severaid (8-24-75) said that 40 percent of us are "incapable of listening." As he expressed it, "We fear an invasion of self."

Observing persons in politics and government leads us to believe the percentage of listening drop-outs in these areas far surpasses that in the general public. It is a rare treat to find a really good listener in public office. Count the ones you have talked to or seen on TV this past year!

In recent years, I (Corinne) have had the opportunity of visiting with a number of legislators in the State Capitol at Sacramento, California. As Legislative Advocate for the California State Division, American Association of University Women, I represented some 30,000 college degree'd women. We were involved in supporting major legislation for women in this state which represents one-tenth of the population of the U.S. And we were deeply involved in working for the ratification of the Equal Rights Amendment which passed in California.

Of the many legislative offices I visited during this time, no more than two or three had what I would judge to be genuine concern for listening as an assertive, positive, absolutely essential activity in connection with their responsibilities to citizens they represented.

One of the best and most efficient listeners at the time was then-Assemblywoman Yvonne Brathwaite Burke (who went on to become a member of the U.S. Congress). She listened intently, and responded with vitality in assisting concerned women to achieve needed legislation at the time.

Another splendid listener, with his own particularly thoughtful style, was Senator Albert S. Rodda, who listened without interruption, save for intelligent questions, for at least thirty minutes to pro arguments on the E.R.A.

Some legislators at the Capitol listened with mild interest or out of a sense of duty. Still others refused to listen at all or avoided being consulted in person.

One legislator, who refused to listen, had made up his mind in advance. "You represent the A.A.U.W.?" he said, with a firm-set jaw. "That's one of those radical women's lib groups like the League of Women Voters, isnt' it?"

What Happens When Faulty Listening Occurs in Government?

How essential listening can be in government is well illustrated by a story found in Theodore H. White's *Breach of Faith.*

It was two weeks before President Nixon would fall.

Fred Buzhardt, special counsel in charge of the now famous tapes, knew what was on them. To quote White: "The first morning conversation of the President, as the tape caught it on June 23rd, 1972, was full of gobbledygook and silences; then came the discussion of routine business —but in between was five minutes of what Buzhardt would later call "this horrible thing.' "

Nixon, according to White, "was still convinced he had done nothing wrong, even after listening to the tapes." He asked Buzhardt to listen to them again. He did, and reported back to Nixon that the tapes made the crime perfectly clear. The President was furious and refused to talk to Buzhardt for a week.

St. Clair, Nixon's attendant defense counsel, had not wanted to listen to the "scratchy sounds of the tapes." Comments White, "He had been unable to afford hours and hours of listening."

Finally, though, on Buzhardt's insistence, St. Clair did listen. A young aide who happened into the room while both men were listening through earphones, recalled St. Clair saying to Buzhardt, "Did you hear that, Fred? I can't believe he said that."

We all know the outcome of that tragic episode. Much of it happened because of faulty listening.

How much time and agony could have been spared all down the line, beginning with the President — who seemed quite incapable of listening to himself and believing what he heard — had the idea of listening's importance been equated with that of talking! Unfortunately, listening — assertive listening — plays a minor role in top level politics or government.

You, as an assertive listener, can have an important impact on politics and government. Here are some of the ways:

How to Influence Politics and Government Through Assertive Listening

First, through analytical listening primarily, you can make better decisions concerning legislation. Attend hearings when major bills are under consideration, if you possibly can. Attend sessions of your legislature to judge for yourself the competency of elected representatives.

How to Influence Politics and Government Through Assertive Listening

On local levels, you, as an assertive listener, should feel responsibility to attend meetings of city and county boards, commissions, and other groups making decisions that concern the public.

To open your mind to new ideas and new personalities, watch candidates on TV or go to observe and listen to them when they appear in public meetings. With your special listening skills, you can better judge than the uninformed person which candidates have basically sound ideas, are "coming on straight," have necessary administrative talent, etc.

Television gives you a marvelous opportunity to observe those running for office, because the camera brings the candidate into your own living room where you can closely observe body language as well as evaluate the spoken message.

Second, as an assertive listener, you can have considerable influence in upgrading the quality of politics and government by working with and for organizations set up to encourage social advocacy.

Examples of such groups include Ralph Nader's Center for Study of Responsive Law, the Corporate Accountability Research Group, and Public Citizens, Inc. According to one of Nader's directors, as reported in *The New Yorker* (Oct. 15, 1973): "Ralph [Nader] wants to get people capable of learning . . . that all they need is themselves . . . and so lead you to make the best use of your energy, education, and talent. He gets you to understand the value of having the right kind of self-confidence — not a know-all sort of self-confidence but the sort that allows you to go into the regulatory agencies, for example, and question the whole system from top to bottom . . . you have to have the fortitude not to be intimidated by . . . experts."

Nader believes that the average citizen in our industrialized society suffers from discouragement about his capacity to make any impact on the forces in his environment which seriously affect his welfare. He encourages active citizenship "to make large institutions more responsive to public needs."

Another group concerned with increasing the citizen's awareness of his or her potential influence is Common Cause, headed by John Gardner. This has been described as "a collection of frustrated citizens" with a dues-paying membership of over 350,000. It is considered the "most effective lobby on campaign finance reform" in Washington. One of Gardner's membership letters warns that Senators and Representatives, whether Republican or Democrat, "are in danger of becoming prisoners of a system dominated by money and secrecy." Members of Common Cause are primarily well-educated and upper-middle-class. They are concerned about opening up "the systems of government and politics to expose how the powerful special interests influence them."

These nobly inspired groups, and others like them, need persons with skill in listening even more than they need talkers.

If more assertive listeners were to demand honesty and integrity in their legislators and officeholders, lessening of control by special interests, and an opening up of government to public scrutiny, we would see a vast improvement in our social system.

As assertive listeners, working individually or with groups, we can influence the upgrading of politics and government by offering honest feedback to what we hear. It is our perfect right to do so, and our responsibility.

A few hundred assertive listeners around the country could work miracles in elevating the status of politics and the stature of government.

Applications

Summary

Good listeners are rare among politicians and persons in government. But tragic episodes in recent history, connected with the Watergate days and the resignation of Nixon, illustrate the need for careful, analytical listening as an important part in the life of any person who is connected with government.

As assertive listeners we can have impact on politics and government through (1) making good judgments about legislation, (2) evaluating candidates for public office, (3) taking an active and participatory interest in legislative processes, and (4) cooperating with influential groups working for better government, such as Common Cause and Ralph Nader's Center for Study of Responsive Law, the Corporate Accountability Research Group, and Public Citizens, Inc.

A few hundred assertive listeners could vastly elevate politics and government in the U.S., using the opportunities at their command.

Assertive listeners can:

Better evaluate legislative proposals than can those with weak listening talent

Make valid judgments about candidates for office

Join groups and organizations working for improvement of government

Participate in the legislative processes on local and national levels as concerned and well informed citizens

Applications

**Listening
in Education**

So Johnny still can't read!

We hear more and more reasons for his problem, which annually worsens despite all the concern, funding, remedial programs, and scolding heaped on poor little Johnny, who wonders why the fuss.

Johnny doesn't suspect, and neither do most of his teachers and his parents, that his reading failure may well be due to very poor, or no, instruction in listening. It's too bad, as someone suggested, that Johnny's ears don't wiggle when he is listening, just as his eyes move when he is reading, so we could tell what is happening inside that little head.

Why Johnny Can't Read

Sara W. Lundsteen, specialist in listening in the classroom, suggests that the earliest of the language skills to appear is listening. She says, ". . . chronologically children listen before they speak, speak before they read, and read before they write."

It follows, then, for improved reading Johnny needs first to learn to listen, not only in the earlier grades, but all the way through elementary and secondary school. Lundsteen emphasizes, ". . . reading may depend so completely upon listening as to appear to be a special extension of listening. What child does not read a selection better after hearing and talking about it? . . . The ability to listen seems to set limits on the ability to read."

"Willy-nilly, the U.S. educational system is spawning a generation of semiliterates," concludes a reporter in a *Newsweek* article. A recent assessment of the writing proficiency of Americans of all ages shows they "tend to use only the simplest sentence structure and the most elementary vocabulary when they write." Essays of 13- and 17-year-olds are "far more awkward, incoherent and disorganized than the same age group's essays of six years ago." The decline in written English is called "only one of many symptoms of a massive 'regression toward the intellectually invertebrate' among American academics."

Why Johnny Can't Write

So Johnny can't read *or* write very well.

What do experts offer as valid reasons for the deterioration in Johnny's writing abilities?

Newsweek summarizes the thinking: "There is no question in the minds of educators that a student who cannot read with true comprehension will never learn to write well. 'Writing is, after all, book-talk,' . . . which 'you learn . . . only by reading.' "

What do experts give as solutions to the problem of poor writing? Courses called "Competence" required of students until they pass (courses focusing on sentence and paragraph structure and elements of style). Writing workshops. Assigned reading and writing based on TV viewing since it is so much a part of the student's life already. And some inner-city schools are teaching English as a "second language."

Concluding, the reporter, *Newsweek's* Merrill Sheils, focuses on the mastery of reading as a basis for writing. "One thing that is clearly needed," he says, "is a renewed emphasis on reading as both a discipline and a diversion."

Again we come back to the realization that listening forms the substructure of all communication. Johnny must read in order to write. Johnny must listen in order to read. (Something could be said about Johnny's speech, which is also pretty faulty in most cases, but that too would require a listening background for improvement.)

Johnny probably can't read OR write very well because he has never really learned to listen. Certainly he has never learned to listen assertively.

Why Doesn't Johnny Listen? The principal reason why Johnny doesn't listen is that his teachers don't know how to teach him to listen. Most of them don't know what listening really is because it has been so poorly defined. (We hope this book may clarify some of the mysteries surrounding listening in all its aspects.)

Of course the school day is crowded. But that is a lame excuse for ignoring listening activity in every subject being taught.

Children are naturally assertive; showing them how they can use their ears to listen in many wonderful ways gives them early confidence in this aspect of their contacts with the outside world.

Presenting listening as an active, exciting, stimulating thing is seldom part of a classroom

agenda. Instead, the general attitude that is developed leads Johnny to think, when you have to
listen, you "have to" and who wants to do what you
HAVE TO?

The teacher who can invent ways to change "have
to listen" to "want to listen" has the problem sol-
ved.

How can a teacher help Johnny want to listen?

First, by presenting him with a role model, by
being a Listening Teacher.

Lundsteen captures the idea well. After completing a learned discourse on listening research in education (still in its infancy), she says the central need "is not to let the child get lost personally. For whether he is an apple polisher or a car washer, each child is crying in his own private wilderness, 'Here I am, care about me, listen to me.' "

The best approach to engaging Johnny in listening activity is to first LISTEN TO JOHNNY. CARE ABOUT HIM.

Three Steps to Better Listening. One little boy who had listened to a record he very much liked in kindergarten said, "That makes my ears happy!"

He summarized the most important thing in presenting any subject any time, anywhere, but especially in early grades, where learning habits are established. Create a receptive attitude.

Applications

Attitudes are readily shaped when things are fun. A good attitude is the first step in learning.

So, how can a teacher make listening fun?

Look to the art educators for leadership in this area of encouraging receptive attitudes. They are creative and have stressed the need for developing children's awareness. They are concerned that children know how things taste and smell, feel and look. They are also concerned that children pay attention to how things sound. Walk into an active modern art class. The creative arts teacher will be motivating children through all their senses, providing unusual sensory experiences. They will be found "playing around" with the smells of spices, perfumes, and flowers; the feel of fur, sandpaper, and fabrics. And somewhere along the line, the children will close their eyes and try identifying sounds — bells, tinkling glass, coins clinking. A creative arts teacher may be whispering a poem to the children as they react with paint or crayon or modeling clay to what it says to them. Another day, the arts teacher will read them a story and the children will make puppets to act it out. Are not all of these fascinating listening experiences?

Ralph Nichols, years ago, in *Are You Listening,* came up with 44 things to do in school to capture children's interest in listening. He suggested whisper games, listening to stories, listening to poetry, and a host of other ideas.

Knowledges are welcome once the attitude is receptive.

Only after the door is open does a child (or anyone else for that matter) really learn anything. Knowledges (we prefer the plural because any learning area has so many types of knowledge) are then in demand.

Just as an experienced teacher will introduce facts and ideas about any subject only after the attitude is receptive, so will the teacher in whatever classroom situation, elementary through secondary and even into college, introduce appropriate knowledges about listening when learners are eager for them.

When the attitude is one of welcome, it is time to show Johnny he can listen in a number of ways, just as he can use his legs to stand on, or to walk, run, or leap.

Skills are willingly practiced when attitudes and knowledges are framed for reference. Most learning experiences fail, especially in the area of skills, because teachers are always getting the cart before the horse. Skills come last, only after attitudes are set and knowledges are a part of the learner.

When listening has been made fun, when its varieties and uses have been made clear, that is the time to practice the skills involved in becoming assertive listeners.

ATTITUDES, KNOWLEDGES, SKILLS — in that order — these are the three magic steps to learning anything. Listening included.

We have assumed that children grow in all their capabilities as they go from one grade to the next. But this isn't necessarily what happens. Certainly it doesn't seem to be happening in listening.

About Listening Failure and False Assumptions

Studies of first-graders show they may be listening to their teachers around 90 percent of the time. But by the time they get to second grade, their listening attention may have sunk to 80 percent. In junior high grades, the percentage may have fallen to less than half, and by high school it has slumped to 28 percent. In college, the listening activity is constantly challenged with the lecture system still so prevalent. But studies show that college freshmen can recall only 50 percent of a 10-minute lecture minutes after they hear it, and two days later they have less than half of this residue!

We have made the false assumption from the beginning of first grade that if a child hears (isn't deaf) he or she is automatically listening. But, as

Dr. Nichols pointed out years ago, "Everyday practice [in listening] does not make us perfect. We may be practicing faults instead of skills!"

We have falsely assumed that, in school, listening will take care of itself. We need to firmly correct that piece of wishful thinking.

We need now to come to a full realization that listening is basic to educational growth — that it does not just happen — and that it can be taught successfully in connection with all subjects within the basic framework of ATTITUDE, KNOWLEDGES, and SKILLS.

We need to view listening as fundamental to the language skills, which, in turn, are basic to all other areas of learning. First, listening. Then speaking. Then reading. Then, with good fortune and some God-given talent, writing!

The listening part of the curriculum will "catch on," however, only when listening is understood as, and presented as, an *assertive activity*. It needs to be far more than a passive acceptance of sound and verbal messages. It must be made a dynamic, controlled, multi-skilled part of human behavior, well within the grasp of every student, and very much wanted by every student.

What's Really Happening With Listening in Schools?
Studies of listening in elementary grades show there are some programs to help children improve listening habits and skills. These have emphasized listening comprehension, auditory perception, and listening to improve "thinking." Tapes

and student workbooks, pre-tests and post-tests, are included in these approaches. Children with bilingual and dialect differences come in for some testing and special listening instruction.

Other approaches to listening include story telling (groups listening to stories and answering true-false questions afterward); creative dramatics; and the use of Listening Centers equipped with all media hardware such as tape recorders, ear phones, and filmstrips.

It is strange, however, that very little study has been made of listening on the high school level, and scant are the contributions to this age group. Up to approximately the seventh-grade level, children seem content to learn through some listening. But then they begin to demand to see the material when it becomes more difficult. "Can I see that?" is the usual request. At this point, reading takes over and listening instruction seems to end. The challenge to continue listening instruction throughout high school has not been met, so we find college freshmen ill equipped to learn by listening — a sad state of affairs when so much of college learning still takes place in the lecture classroom.

Colleges are including listening comprehension units in most communication programs. They have discovered that teaching of reading did not result in students being taught how to listen, as Dr. Lundsteen has emphasized. So some corrective measures are undertaken in college. But, by then, learning habits are established and it is difficult to build new ones.

There is a nationwide need for greatly improved methods of teaching listening, keeping it alive, from pre-school through college. Even more, there is the need to redefine what is meant by listening itself. Instead of limiting it to a skill which relates only to a better understanding of what is heard (nothing wrong in that, of course), listening must be broadened to include all of the benefits resulting from what we call Assertive Listening: e.g., better understanding of the *intended* message, better understanding of the *other person* and his or her needs, retention of *desired* information and ideas, *freedom to discard* useless input, *motivation* for creative projects and ideas, and improvement of *communication* with others and with one's self.

When Will Johnny Learn to Really Listen?

There is a wonderful, true story not generally known about how long it took to rid the English sailors of the plague of scurvy, although the secret of scurvy prevention lay just across the English channel. Listen:

In 1564, Dutch vessels had NO scurvy. They had printed materials containing information about the need for fresh fruit and vegetables.

In 1595, 31 years later, the English publication, *Surgeon's Mate,* first carried a news item of this marvelous preventative.

In 1601, six years later, an English sea captain got around to advocating compulsory rations of fresh fruit or vegetables, but 16 years after that, in 1617, the first appropriation for this ration was suggested.

Then, in 1754, 137 years later, the first study of scurvy was made and 20 different varieties discovered.

In 1795, 41 years later, English ships were at long last provided with a compulsory ration of fruits and vegetables, and no deaths from scurvy were reported from that time on.

How long did it take to get the news across the channel? It took 231 years and, in the meantime, 20,000 English sailors died of scurvy!

When will Johnny be taught assertive listening right from the beginning of school? Let us hope educators will realize the need for it in all the grades, to overcome the scourge of semiliterates with their lack of communication adequacy.

Let us hope it takes far less than 231 years to end the annual loss of thousands of potentially good students, like Johnny, who can't read, can't write, and can't really communicate — all because they have never learned how to listen.

Summary

Listening comes before speaking, reading, and writing, in that order, according to specialists in listening in the classroom. But the U.S. educational system is built on a curriculum plan that neglects listening and endeavors to encourage reading and writing without sufficient emphasis on, or background in, the natural progression of communication from listening to speaking, to reading, to writing.

Children fail to develop listening expertise because of a lack of Listening Teachers as role models, who understand what listening really is.

In correcting the present situation, and in teaching listening in the classroom, teachers need to pay attention to the natural learning process, which starts with the development of (1) receptive attitudes, and is followed by (2) presentation of needed knowledges, followed by (3) emphasis on skills.

We have falsely assumed that listening in school will take care of itself. Teaching listening as an assertive, positive, creative activity should start in the elementary grades and carry throughout the curriculum, in all grades, and in all subjects.

Teaching assertive listening in education:

Should begin in pre-school and carry on throughout the elementary and secondary grades, and should be emphasized in all subject areas.

Should begin with a listening teacher as effective role model

Should precede speaking, reading, and writing, in that order, to correlate with the natural progression of communication learning in the human being

**Listening
for Pleasure**

Listen to this poetic invention of a six-year-old English girl:

"The dustmans van came lumbering down
Bumpety, Bumpety Bump the cars came rackling
Down the street chacl chacl chacl I
Never got use to the market on Monday
mandy morning."

Obviously, her listening pleasure has not been ruined by a world that imposes dictionary words, correctly spelled and combined into sentences, grammatically pristine. Yet, as Robert Nye, writing the *Christian Science Monitor* on "Songs of Innocents," says: "Every child of six is a poet, but at six it is too easy . . . children are alive to language . . . delight in the shape and sound of words. . . ." And he comments on the problems of keeping the childlike enjoyment in sounds of words, often invented words, until one grows into adulthood. "To preserve the capacity to see things new, while knowing them old," he says, "is the difficult and wonderful thing." We could add that preserving the capacity to *hear* things new, while knowing them old — that is also a most wonderful thing.

How Do You Listen for Pleasure?

Have you tried:
Placing a seashell to your ear to hear ocean waves slapping the shore?
Listening to bees buzzing outside your window on a lazy, summer day?
Listening to a baby babbling its contented sounds?
Going to hear a great symphony?
Going to a rock concert?

If you have done all of these, you have tried a nice range of sounds — from those you hear with your inner ear only to those so loud you almost have to plug your ears to stand them. (Some rock artists do plug their ears, the sound is so intense.)

At times a very tiny sound can stir up greater plea-   **Quiet Sounds**
sure in some listeners than a massive sound. Take, for example, listening to a clavichord.

There is the story of the man who had no background in listening to this ancient keyboard instrument in which the strings are so softly struck with metal blades that the sound is very faint.

When he first heard the clavichord, he said to his more knowledgeable friend, "Wouldn't it be a great idea to amplify this sound? We could place a microphone beside the keyboard and it would come up loud and clear. You could hear it way at the back of a big hall."

"Ah," said his friend, "true. But that would destroy the pleasure of the clavichord completely. The delight in this instrument is having to LISTEN to hear it."

Sometimes, you don't even need sound to listen for pleasure.

Edgar Lee Masters, the poet, spoke of many kinds of silences he had known — "the silence of the stars and of the sea,/ And the silence of the city when it pauses,/ And the silence of a man and a maid. . . ." He recalls the silence of "great love" and "deep peace of mind" and "the silence of age,/ Too full of wisdom for the tongue to utter it/ In words intelligible to those who have not lived/ The great range of life."

And then, of course, there is that poetic fragment of poet Rod McKuen, who speaks for the inner poet in many a modern man or woman:

". . . lie down in the darkness and listen to the warm."

Musical Sounds   Recently we (Geetings) attended a concert featuring two extraordinary musical experiences, in complete contrast but equally exciting to the trained ear.

It was a symphony concert, and programmed was Mozart's Piano Concerto in C Minor, K. 491, with a distinguished British pianist. The contrasting selection was Gustav Mahler's Symphony No. 5 in C Sharp Minor.

The critic, reviewing these juxtaposed experiences, revealed the feelings of the audience as it listened, almost as one body.

"The Mozart Concerto," said the critic, "is one of his greatest — one quality seemed to shine above all [in the performance] — the way it can range from the most sophisticated fascinations, to the kind of childlike simplicity that only a few great geniuses (like Mozart) seem capable of in their maturity. . . ."

The guest pianist was praised for his "brilliance . . . always under control . . . strong when he had to be without ever sounding even slightly percussive." But the critic continued, "Of all the admirable things he did, I admired most the tenderness he brought to the childlike pathos of the slow movement. . . ."

Turning then to the Mahler, the critic said of the seventy-five minute symphony, "The work is *a fascinating example of music as human communication,* the more fascinating because unlike a number of other Mahler symphonies, it has no 'program' . . . it tells a kind of emotional 'story' as clearly and powerfully as any words could . . . the story of an emotional progress from dark to light . . . from the depths of a fierce sorrow . . . to a happy, excited joy . . ." (Emphasis ours.)

The critic, adept with words, was able to recall verbally almost exactly the emotional experience the audience had enjoyed in listening to these two remarkable and completely different musical works. Of course, this critic is an assertively trained musical listener, hearing sounds from a well developed background (frame of reference).

How different the experience would have been for someone lacking all musical understanding! (For-

tunately, in the case of the concert we have referred to, the audience was made up largely of
regular symphony goers). The untrained person,
on hearing Mahler's mournful cellos and brilliant
French horn and trumpet, might have been
perplexed at the contrasts and climaxes and sudden hushes and changing rhythms. He might
even have found them distasteful. Or, worse yet,
boring!

A hard rock concert can be quite another thing.
Here the intensity of sound, far beyond anything to
come out of a symphony concert, is almost overwhelming to the uninitiated. For those who have
developed a taste for rock, a concert can be a
tremendously moving experience.

Music is all in the ear of the listener, and an assertively trained ear can stretch its acceptance
widely to find elements of pleasure in all types of
musical sound.

Poetic Sounds

Listening to poetry being read aloud (even beauti-
fully) can be a very trying experience to the untrained ear. It can be a dynamic and thrilling experience for the listener who has built up an appreciation for poetry in all its dimensions. There is
pleasure in poetry, from the briefest light verse
couplet to the full-evening, poetry concert.

The late Scott Buchanan, considered one of the
great teachers of our century, said in one of his
famous conversations about teaching, as he
commented on poetry in primary and secondary

school: "There should be a great deal of poetry to get the imagination wakened and moving easily." He reminded us that "poetry is the oldest of the written — even the spoken — disciplines. Even before there was writing," he said, "there was poetry."

As a result of the failure in schools to provide listening opportunities for children to hear poetry read (or to make up their own poetry, free of ties to dictionaries, grammar, and sentence structure!), there is a general lack of interest in poetry among American adults. Poetry is hard to sell. There is scant market for it. Buchanan remarked that, in planning big bi-weekly lectures for the public in the Great Hall at Cooper Union (which he did for several years), "It seemed to me the ordinary adult audience was missing in poetic understanding."

To prepare yourself to listen with pleasure to poetry, it is necessary to build some frame of reference through conscientiously listening with all the assertive powers at your command (listening analytically, listening to learn, listening creatively, and even with Tender Loving Care) to recordings and tapes and to live performers who are always around in coffeehouses and on campuses, searching for audiences.

Poetry covers a world of listening experiences. Somewhere you will find a place to tune in and begin listening with pleasure, a place where your present understanding can fit into the poetic world.

Once converted, you will find unusual pleasure in the shape and sound of words, thoughts and feelings to be found only in the world of poetry.

Other Sounds

The world of pleasure through sound, non-verbal as well as verbal, is limited only by your imagination.

Even without moving now, you can close your eyes and in memory recall sounds of childhood, as did Wallace Stegner. While, in his memorable story of recalling the smell of wolf willow, he placed emphasis on the one link that brought the past to him ("pungent and pervasive, the smell that has always meant my childhood"), he also recalled the old pump. "For an instant my teeth are on edge with the memory of the dry screech of that pump before a dipperful of priming water took hold . . . and I dipped a bucket down into the hold in the ice and toted it, staggering . . . up the dugway to the kitchen door."

What sounds of childhood can you reconstruct in your mind's ear?

You can extend your listening pleasure beyond anything now imaginable.

Where can you start, once you have dealt with your childhood listening pleasures?

Just for the fun of it, pull out any cut glass pieces you might have in the cupboard. Line them up and thump them lightly with your fingers or a silver spoon. Listen to the delightful variety of pitches.

Tonight, after dark, go out and listen to the night sounds. Do you hear distant cars? Crickets? Someone's hi-fi playing Mozart or Mahler or Rock? Do you hear a 747 racing through the sky?

Now, tomorrow, just for good measure, somewhere find a clavichord if you can. If you can't, borrow or buy a recording or tape of one. Curiosity should get you that far, at least, on the road to new listening pleasures.

And finally, somewhere, find a place where there is absolutely no sound. None at all! And listen to the silence, for, as the poet said,

"Silence is the speech of love,
The music of the spheres above . . ."

Summary

All children have within them creativity which, if preserved and nourished throughout their maturing process, can lead to great enjoyment of stimuli coming through the senses throughout life. Great poems, works of music, works of art, have been stimulated by the various senses, including hearing (listening).

To develop pleasure by assertively listening in a creative way, you are encouraged to try all types of poetry readings, dramatic presentations, and other performances emphasizing sound. Also you are encouraged to develop your sensitivity to natural sounds. Your creativity can extend the many ways in which you can listen for pleasure. Your world of pleasant sound is limited only by your imagination.

Assertive listeners have learned to:

Listen for pleasure to all types of performances — musical, dramatic, poetic, etc.

Listen for pleasure to all manner of natural sounds — bees buzzing to birds chirping

Creatively explore listening as a source of motivation for works of the imagination

Enjoy listening to silence, "the music of the spheres"

**Listening
to Your Selves**

At last we come to a consideration of the most fascinating of all subjects — YOURSELF.

Someone who had observed much about the Self once said: "We are populous with unrealized selves; with might-have-beens; with partially-weres; with sometimes-ares; with may-yet-bes."

Are you? Of course you are!

Take your might-have-beens. Might you have been a revolutionist? A Phi Beta Kappa? A great actress? Lawyer? Criminal?

Think about your partially-weres. Did you, temporarily, fulfill the role of compatible husband or wife? Rebel against authority and almost become a revolutionary? Miss by a year or two finishing your law degree?

How about your sometimes-ares? Sometimes are you a good guy or sweetheart" and at others a crank? Sometimes are you an inspired cook and at others a TV-dinner drudge? Sometimes are you utterly charming and at other times a monumental bore?

Ah! But what about your may-yet-bes? Are you young, with most of your life unmapped? May you become a host of glamorous things — actor, politician, who knows — even President? Are you in your late seventies or eighties? If so, let's hope you haven't ruled out your vista of may-yet-bes!

How to find out about yourself — your selves, rather?

To continue the quote with which we began: ". . .
The terms of your own equipment are the only
terms in which anything can reach you."

Undoubtedly the worst equipment most of us have
for self-discovery, self-analysis, self-
understanding, and self-development is the ear in
all its aspects and psychological extensions —
what many have referred to as "the inner ear."
Unfortunately, also, some sentimental potboilers
on the virtues of listening to oneself have made the
subject about as palatable as sticky cotton candy.

That does not negate the desperate need each of
us has to listen to our selves with the expertise we
have developed for listening to others.

Know Thyself

The assertive listener, directing new-found skills to
the self, is favorably equipped to do what Socrates
advised all of us to do: KNOW THYSELF.

How did Socrates plan to do this for himself?

By asking questions of everyone he met, and by
observing how he — Socrates — in his own mind
reacted to them. He was willing to risk discovering
his own being. So dedicated was he to this task,
we are told, that he was never known to show the
slightest resentment or anger when an argument
was turned against him.

Socrates began adult life by trying to master his father's trade of sculpting. He did very well, but he yanked off his apron and threw down his tools at age thirty-five and turned to sculpting thoughts, which he had decided were more real than something one could get out of a block of marble.

Socrates felt that, above all things, we need to remain self-centered (not to be equated with selfish), and in this respect his thinking is quite up-to-date at a time when psychologists, psychiatrists, psychotherapists, semanticists, and all the other "ists" are agreed on one core idea: self-acceptance is basic to good relationships with others.

Dr. Carl Rogers, one of America's most distinguished psychologists, is speaking of learnings which have affected him personally when he says, *"I find I am more effective when I can listen acceptantly to myself, and can be myself."* He further says he believes that "we cannot change, we cannot move away from what we are, until we thoroughly *accept* what we are. Then change seems to come about almost unnoticed."

Upon knowing himself and listening to himself "acceptantly," Dr. Rogers explains his relationships with others then become real. And, "Real relationships tend to change rather than to remain static."

As he accepts himself, Rogers says he is able to permit himself to *"understand another person."* Then, "If I let myself really understand another person, I might be changed by that understanding."

To start on a hopeful note, it is true that most of us find, when we finally get to know our selves, we are better than we had thought we were. Despite the treatment we may have received in childhood (leading us to believe we were hardly OK), the strict religious doctrines that left no doubt we were "born in sin," and academic grades that left us questioning our mental or creative potential — despite all these, the more we listen to our selves the more positive we become in acceptance of our selves. Negative attitudes toward self tend to decrease. In client-centered therapy, says Dr. Rogers, this quiet penetration of self results in the often disturbed person coming to *"like* himself" and taking pleasure in *being* himself.

Getting to Know Your Selves

To continue on a hopeful note, we know that the capacity of the human being for change is fairly limitless. We are not boxed in to many unchangeable, unalterable personal traits we don't like. We can do something to improve, and each day the research being carried on in human behavior brings us news of new means of altering and improving it. TM and its various approaches, investigations in the "powers of mind," better foods, exercise programs — they all have a bearing on improving the self. They all deserve careful investigation to see how they can help you with your needs as revealed in listening to your selves.

**Break Out
of Your Cocoon**

Wendell Johnson, in *People in Quandaries,* gave us a number of ideas worth constant re-examination.

Heed one of the best: "Quandaries . . . are rather like verbal cocoons in which individuals elaborately encase themselves, and from which, under circumstances common in our time, they do not tend to hatch."

Most of us are in varying states of quandary, due largely to the cocoons of belief in which we have wrapped ourselves. "I am too short" — "I am stupid" — "I am very smart" — "I am highly talented — "I have a terrible voice, nobody wants to listen to." *I AM* is the great creator of myths, stereotypes, and rigid concepts that shape cocoons from which there is limited escape. But escape is possible.

In breaking loose from such a cocoon, we must understand that the verb "To Be" and its various forms (I am, I am not, I will be, etc.) tend to cause a catastrophic range of problems. Once we have told the self, "I am too fat," it is hard to break loose from a projection of fat forever.

"Just as little drops of water will wear away a rock, so many little 'is's' will wear away a hope," said Wendell Johnson while warning against the frequent and careless use of "To Be."

It helps, as you ponder cocoon problems, to substitute "appear" or "seem" to hear what happens. "I appear overweight" isn't so hard to listen to as "I am fat," is it? It leaves the door open for change.

In any case, be aware of the cocoon in which you have already encased yourself, and start breaking out of it to prepare for self-listening.

We speak about YOURSELF. But what we really mean, in tune with modern technology, is YOUR SELVES. We started by suggesting the many unrealized selves, the several potential selves we all have living within our bodies.

Multiple Selves — How Many Have You?

Each one of us has more than one self, when we start peeling off the protective layers.

Dr. Samuel J. Bois, in *The Art of Awareness,* has compared the "objective somebody that looks very much like us" that we see as we come out of our skin and look back in, to an actor who plays the main part in our drama of life.

But wait! Behind the actor is the observer of the
play, who reacts to the actor. Behind them is the
director, who makes decisions about what to do
and how to do it. Then another person appears, to
discuss the whole play with us.

Self, in Bois' drama, becomes four persons (more
are possible). "Self-1 is the actor; Self-2 is the observer; Self-3 is the director of the play; Self-4 is
the theorizer."

Extending this idea of Selves, we could say that
Self-1 is the front man or woman. Self-1 meets
friends in the grocery store, goes to the office,
carries out all predictable tasks of living. Self-1
frequently has what others call our "charming personality" or our "hostile nature."

Self-2 goes deeper. This is the aware one, constantly observing and picking up ideas, reacting
emotionally to everything happening "out there." If
we are creative, Self-2 is very active, picking up on
stimuli — much of it, of course, from listening.

"Unless our Self-2 keeps functioning, observing,
and inventing ceaselessly," says Bois, "we quickly
become has-beens in a world that keeps on bury-
ing the past and building the future."

Self-3 comes close to being the inner assertive
listener who finally evaluates all new knowledge,
experience, information "he gathers from reading,
listening, or meditating" and directs Self-2. Self-3
is the final guide, judge, or Adult, who gives YOU
integrity, stability, and direction.

Self-4 may appear at times to carry on a philosophical discussion to find the meaning of it all, if we are blessed with a thoughtful and metaphysical nature.

In listening to your selves, it helps to realize what you observe on the surface in Self-1 — "too fat" — "stupid" — "homely" — is but the outer layer. What you hear when Self-1 says "Hi, how are you?" at the grocery store or office is the front person's welcome.

Communicating With Your Selves

But listen to that person. Self-1 is presenting you to others.

How does Self-1 sound?

To get the sound of the voice, we used to put our heads into a corner and talk. Or we would cup the mouth and ear together with our hands to get the sound. Now we can hear ourselves on tape, but it is often a shock to hear one's voice, as others hear it, for the first time.

"Do I really sound like that?" is the customary reaction.

Listening to one's own voice, though, is important. Do I sound nasal, too loud, is the pitch offensive to others? Is my diction clear?

If improvement is indicated, it is available and possible. Age, general physical condition, emotional life — all these influence the sound of the voice others listen to when you open your mouth to speak.

Sometimes fear of illness may cause psychosomatic deterioration of vocal quality. An example of this is a fellow who, as a young man, had built an enviable reputation for his clarity and tonal quality in much public speaking for political causes. He had become known as the boy "with the million dollar voice."

As he grew older, his resonant tones fell by the wayside. No one noticed his beautiful voice. Something seemed to be happening in his throat; his larynx was deteriorating, he felt sure.

So he went to a throat specialist who examined him and said absolutely nothing was wrong. He relaxed and looked into improving his general health through good diet, rest, and exercise.

Miraculously, almost, "the million dollar voice" returned. Somewhat older-sounding, to be sure. But worthy of special note. You hear it quite often on TV or radio. It belongs to a man now over 70 but still strong and able in body, mind, and voice.

In addition to noting how Self-1 sounds, you will also want to use your powers as assertive listener to note how Self-1 comes across in the various aspects of body and face language we have discussed.

Is Self-1 making the contact with others pleasant and agreeable? Does Self-1, in appearance, say what you want him or her to say about YOU?

In each way that you listen to your selves, going from Self-1 to Self-2 and Self-3 (and possibly Self-4, if you have such), start by freeing your total self of guilt for taking such interest in YOU.

You owe it to your selves to get to know them in all the ways you can listen to them — for information; analytically, to discover their needs; with Tender Loving Care; and, of course, creatively.

In each episode of listening, recall the five basic steps of the assertive listening process, discussed in Part I. Remember: (1) Rule out either-or judgment and open your mind to full-color input. (2) Observe words and word patterns you are using inside — are you talking to your selves and listening to your selves with the same word meanings? (3) Observe all aspects of body and face language as you listen. (4) Make careful evaluations of the messages you receive from your selves. And finally, when you come to (5), remember your perfect right as assertive listener to chart the map of your territory, your improvement, or, as we often say, create your own "Self-Fulfilling Prophecies."

Do you know all there is to know about your selves already?

By now you know, we are sure, that *assuming* you know all about your selves is no way to start. Open your mind to new understandings. Be on the alert for the unexpected, even if, at first, it is unacceptable.

On Listening to Learn About Your Selves

No doubt you know how much you weigh, your height, your general state of health. Do you listen to your surface self (Self-1), to your general "personality," to hear how you can improve voice, tone quality, and also shorten and enliven your oral output? Do you observe Self-1 as it listens to others? Is it attentive, relaxed, patient, kind; or tense, critical and judgmental?

As you go deeper, do you listen to Self-2 to find out what has been learned today through reading, listening, observing? Do you practice one of the several valuable forms of meditation? Do you stop Self-1 from talking, long enough to let Self-2 receive valuable stimuli?

Coming to your Self-3, the judge, do you listen carefully to your Adult self to find how the stimuli can lead into a better life for you in some way, enrich your contacts with others, motivate possibly a creative project that has a possibility of success?

If you have a deep inner Self-4 of philosophical tendency, do you take the time to listen to hidden meanings?

On Listening Creatively to Your Selves

As you pick up courage to listen in depth to your selves, you will hear, especially in Self-2, your Child demanding some playtime. You will always find yourself feeling some guilt in this area of listening because you were trained to "make use of your time," "work hard physically," etc., etc. But your value system may now be altered to encompass what you formerly rejected — more time for creative living. Your methods of thinking and reacting may rise to new dimensions of creative life. Assertively listening to creative needs you have, may help you break the hold "the old order" has on you.

As Ghiselin Brewster says in *The Creative Process,* "Before any new order can be defined, the absolute power of the established, the hold upon us of what we know and are, must be broken."

Look for new thrills in life as you learn to listen to your selves creatively!

**On Listening
With TLC
to Your Selves**

Harold Blake Walker, in *To Conquer Loneliness,* reports the story of a little child playing alone, quite happily, in her back yard. A neighbor called to ask where her mother was. "Mom's asleep," the child said.

"Well," the neighbor continued, "where's your little brother?"

"He's asleep too," said the contented child.

Whereupon the neighbor said, "Aren't you lonesome, playing all by yourself?"

"No," the child answered honestly. "I like me."

Walker makes this observation: "If we are able to like ourselves, to respect ourselves, we are able to cope with aloneness. It is the cracks in character, the self-will and selfishness, and our unlovable ways, that make and keep the inscape lonely and isolated from others. . . ."

Listening to your selves — all of them — with Tender Loving Care is not a selfish act. On the other hand, it is a very necessary thing, and will be your greatest gift to others. In the process you may discover you have some unlovable qualities. But if you do, fine. Take measures to remedy these. "If the inscape is tortured by conflict, the landscape of people is inescapably alien. . . . If we are unable to accept ourselves we cannot believe we are accepted by others."

Be a patient, kind, tolerant, helpful, encouraging, very quiet assertive listener to your selves, periodically. You will find hidden anxieties and worries, hidden emotions and feelings, needing your listening attention. Give them your best Tender Loving Care.

On Listening Analytically to Your Selves

Now comes the intense assertive listening. This takes great courage, especially when you are so apt to find discouraging facts. Take heart! One thing we know, you can change behavior.

There are danger signals indicating deep inner problems that surface in Self-1. Listen analytically for them. Here are some of those signals:

Incessant talking. Do you talk far too much? Oral hemophilia is a primary offender in modern society. Especially offensive long-term talking is also accompanied by emotional display, loaded words, and angry body language. Still, some persons just talk quietly in a murderous monotone. Taking up more than your share of total communication time should give you pause to consider what inner turmoil is threatening to become distress (if it hasn't reached that stage already).

Giving lots of advice. Do you hear yourself saying "You should do this" or "That is the only way to go"? Stop to realize your intentions, no matter how pure, are subject to misinterpretation. Such statements tend to expose you as a person who likes overpowering others, imposing ideas on the world. Often, this tendency to tell others what to do comes out of a weak, insecure inner person.

Talking in generalities. Do you hear yourself say things like "Religion is an outmoded thing in this society; we ought to close all churches." Or, "Freedom is a thing of the past." Or, "Motherhood is highly overrated." These types of generalities are danger signals. You are presenting a picture of a person whose thinking is shallow, opinionated, and not to be taken seriously.

Fabricating, misquoting, identifying incorrectly. Alarming statements full of unsubstantiated "facts" and misquotes may grab the attention, but for reasons you do not intend. They tell assertive listeners you are an exhibitionist, more interested in showing off than in contributing to meaningful communication.

Asking loaded questions. The old loaded question, "When did you stop beating your wife?" can't be improved on by way of illustration here. Do you listen to the questions you ask others? Are they designed to serve as traps? Or are they designed to do what questions should in terms of gathering information about who, what, where, when, and how much? Or perhaps for the purpose of encouraging others to listen to themselves, as in the case of TLC listening?

Interrupting others. Probably the most unforgivable habit one can acquire is that of interrupting others. Do you start to talk before the other person is finished? Do you constantly finish sentences for others? Such behavior indicates a desire to control that is beyond control. If you hear yourself interrupting, consider it a danger signal of deeper trouble.

On "Self-Fulfilling Prophecies" and Other Resources

Carl Rogers said, "The emotionally maladjusted person . . . is in difficulty first because communication within himself has broken down, and second because as a result of this his communication with others has been damaged."

All that we have been saying in this book is summarized in that sentence; however, negatively. Let us reverse the thought and say that the emotionally adjusted person is stable and self-actualizing, first because communication within himself is flourishing, and second because as a result of this his communication with others is excellent.

In listening to yourself, if you sense a breakdown in your communication system with either yourself or others (because of it), you have several possible aids, including these:

You can seek professional advice, analysis, and help. If you find it difficult to listen to your selves well enough to ascertain your true inner needs, likes and dislikes, strengths and weaknesses, you can seek diagnostic testing at your local colleges or universities (when available) or ask for help from a professional counselor. There are a number of good tests that can tell you a lot about yourself — your special talents, interests, and desires. One of the best is the Strong-Campbell, a diagnostic instrument, non-sex oriented, which will surprise you with its capacity to listen to your inner selves, telling you what areas of special interest, concern, and adaptability are yours. If you are enrolled in an educational institution, find what is available to you now at the counselor's office.

Another source of reliable "listening" and counseling is often your minister, rabbi, or priest. Many of these men and women are well trained to offer you help and to listen to you and your selves talk. Many of them are well equipped to do the finest kind of listening, keyed to your special needs.

You can formulate policies which will be self-fulfilling. Finally, as you discover areas of needed improvement within your selves, through listening, you can shape policies to correct your weaknesses and fortify your strengths. Put these in the form of prophecies: "By this time next year, I will be able to enjoy being in a group without talking all the time. I will have the self-control to know I am not being weak by taking the part of a good listener. I will be an assertive listener, fully active and prepared to direct myself and the group, if need be, by sharpening my awareness of the total communication."

You will want to make your own policies and your own prophecies, realizing that, if you believe in them, they will come true.

By this time next week, I will be a better listener, not only to others, but to myself. That is a good prophecy to start on. If you believe it when you say it, chances are very good that it will be "self-fulfilling."

Take it a step at a time.

But never doubt that you can win friends, mellow enemies, help loved ones, and change your own life through developing your powers of assertive listening.

Summary

The most fascinating of all subjects is YOURSELF. But in listening, we discover we have several selves. We have at least three (Self-1, the actor; Self-2, the observer; and Self-3, the director of the play). If we are very self-actualizing, we have a fourth Self, the theorizer.

In getting to KNOW OUR SELVES we do well to analyze the sound of our own voices by listening to them on tapes (making needed improvements in tone quality, diction, and pronunciation); freeing ourselves of guilt in addressing the inner selves — 1, 2, 3, and possibly 4 — for closer scrutiny. Being self-acceptant is the basis of becoming an effective communicator, and especially of becoming a good multi-purposeful assertive listener.

We need to learn periodically to listen to our selves in all the ways we have discussed in this book: For Information, Analytically, with Tender Loving Care, and Creatively. Establishing helpful "self-fulfilling prophecies" to correct bad listening habits and encourage the best of listening habits in the future, is a good way to start an improvement in listening expertise. One step at a time! One step at a time! One step at a time! That will take us to "greener pastures" in winning friends, mellowing enemies, helping loved ones, and changing our own lives through assertive listening.

To listen to our selves we need to:

First, know our selves – our inner selves as well as the surface self

Use all the skills described and analyzed in this book

Become self-acceptant, eliminating feelings of self-guilt and self-criticism

Establish workable step-by-step "self-fulfilling prophecies" for self-improvement